# Embracing Writing

## The First-Year Writing Program at Bridgewater State College

Second Edition

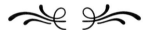

Anne Doyle
Benjamin Carson
Michelle Cox
Kathryn Evans
Evelyn Pezzulich
*Bridgewater State College*

KENDALL/HUNT PUBLISHING COMPANY
4050 Westmark Drive     Dubuque, Iowa 52002

Cover images provided by the authors.

Copyright © 2006, 2007 by Anne Doyle, Benjamin Carson, Michelle Cox, Kathryn Evans, and Evelyn Pezzulich

ISBN 978-0-7575-4536-8

Printed in the United States of America
10 9 8 7 6 5 4 3 2 1

Dedicated with respect and appreciation to the
adjunct faculty of the English Department
at Bridgewater State College

# ❧ Contents ❧

# To the Student

*Embracing Writing* will be useful to you in several ways as you develop as a writer in BSC's writing program. The goals of the writing program include developing nuanced and meaningful arguments; locating, evaluating, integrating, and documenting primary and secondary sources to support your arguments; focusing and organizing your writing; moving through the processes of writing—inventing, composing, revising, editing, and proofreading—according to the conventions of standard written English; and composing in a voice appropriate to the audience and purpose of your writing.

You may find the following features of this book to be especially helpful:

- **A list of important resources.** These resources include the Writing Studio, where experienced consultants can give you feedback on your work before you turn it in. As a client in the Writing Studio, you may bring in work you have written independently or work you have written for a class—any class, not just an English class. The Writing Studio is a useful resource in helping you fine-tune your work not only before you submit it to your professor, but also before you submit it for publication in one of BSC's many journals. In addition to the Writing Studio, the list of resources includes the counseling center; technological resources, including many that are useful but little-known; and the library, which can help you in more ways than you may realize.

- **A list of places you can publish and present your work.** BSC students have important things to say—things that are worthy of reaching a larger audience. In addition, publishing or presenting your work looks good on your résumé and is personally gratifying.

- **A section on helpful strategies for writing.** The strategies described in this section will help you to write even more effectively.

- **Essays written by ENGL 101 and 102 students.** In addition to being interesting reading, each essay features an introduction that discusses the rhetorical strategies used by the writer—strategies that you may want to use in your own writing. Two of the essays also feature annotations (notes in the margins) illustrating the criteria many instructors will use when grading your work. Having these illustrations at your disposal may help you produce even better work.

- **A blank calendar for you to note all your due dates, including those in other classes.** Being able to see all your due dates in one place not only helps you remember them but also helps you more deliberately manage your time, especially when you have two papers or exams on the same day or only a few days apart. You'll find your calendar at the end of the book, just before the submission information for next year's *Embracing Writing*.

- **The submission and award information that you'll need when you submit your work for consideration in next year's *Embracing Writing*.** You'll find this information on the last page of this book.

# To the Instructor

*Embracing Writing* is designed to support the goals of the first-year writing program at Bridgewater State College and to familiarize readers with BSC's writing program and resources.

You may find four features of this book to be especially helpful:

- **Outcomes that students are expected to have achieved by the end of 101 and 102, along with the CONNECT rubric providing more detail about these outcomes.** The outcomes and rubric may be helpful to use or adapt as criteria when you assign writing, and they may also be helpful when giving students feedback on their work.

- **A list of places for students to publish and present their work.** When students are encouraged or required to share their work with a broader audience, many instructors find that their work is better; the prospect of a broader audience often motivates students to spend more time crafting their writing.

- **Helpful strategies for writing.** This section provides four sets of concrete strategies that your students can use to revise more effectively.

- **A selection of readings written by previous 101 and 102 students, including headnotes and annotations highlighting the strengths of those works.** Students enjoy reading work written by people they can identify with, and the headnotes will help them focus their reading on rhetorical strategies that they may find useful in their own writing. In addition, two of the readings are annotated to highlight especially effective rhetorical strategies—strategies that may help your students submit better work to you.

# Mission Statement

The mission of the first-year writing program at Bridgewater State College is to teach students the conventions of writing in the college classroom and to demonstrate the importance of critical reading and writing beyond the classroom as students enter into communities and become responsible, concerned citizens. Because the work students undertake in both ENGL 101: Writing I and ENGL 102: Writing II is important to nearly all other classes they will take at Bridgewater State College, it makes sense that both courses are taken in the first year.

All of the writing that students do is undertaken against a backdrop of a classroom alive with texts: texts that students create and texts of published writers. Reading has a central role in first-year writing classes. A substantial part of Writing I is devoted to helping students become better readers of their own writing as well as the writing of others. Conversations about writing, reading, and literacy focus on the rhetorical effects of argument on readers and writers as people in the world.

The balance between preparing students for college level writing and developing critical literacy among new college writers is the constant concern of faculty teaching the courses. Each class works differently to reflect that balance in the nature and number of writing assignments presented in the classroom, but all of them reflect particular shared outcomes for each course.

## A Word about the Connect Writing Project

Connect is a partnership among five public institutions of higher education: Bristol Community College, Cape Cod Community College, Massasoit Community College, Bridgewater State College, and the University of Massachusetts at Dartmouth. One major aim of the Connect partnership is to enhance academic programs and ease the transfer of students among the institutions. To help achieve this goal, the Connect Writing Project was formed to create common outcomes for first-year writing courses at the five institutions of higher learning.

# Outcomes for First-Year Writing Courses

## ENGL 101: Writing I

Students will do the following:

- move through the processes of writing: inventing, composing, revising, and editing according to the conventions of Standard Written English*
- critically read and respond to a variety of texts, including their own*
- compose in a voice appropriate to the audience and the purpose of writing*
- formulate a thesis and support it with evidence*
- compose coherent and cohesive essays and other texts*
- learn various organizational structures of the expository essay

## ENGL 102: Writing II

Students will do the following:

- continue to develop all of the skills fostered in ENGL 101 Writing I
- understand that research consists of a series of tentative hypotheses that are then tested and affirmed or revised
- locate, evaluate, integrate, and document secondary source materials to support a position, including electronic sources*
- learn the written forms of accepted academic research
- become familiar with the conventions of citation appropriate to various disciplines

*Those outcomes marked by an asterisk are Connect Writing Project outcomes for first-year composition and are held in common by Bristol Community College, Cape Cod Community College, Bridgewater State College, Massasoit Community College, and the University of Massachusetts at Dartmouth.

On the following page you will find a common CONNECT rubric for evaluating writing.

# Connect Group: Writing Outcomes and Rubrics

| | Writing: Students will move through the processes of writing, including inventing, composing, revising, and editing | Critical reading: Students will read and respond to a variety of texts | Audience, purpose, voice: Students will compose in a voice appropriate to the audience and purpose of the writing | Thesis: Students will formulate a thesis and support it with evidence | Organization: Students will compose coherent and cohesive texts | Research, documentation: Students will obtain, evaluate, and document primary and/or secondary source materials to support a position |
|---|---|---|---|---|---|---|
| **Novice** | Writing shows little change from invention to final draft, despite consistent problems with content and/or editing. | Writing demonstrates poor comprehension of relevant texts, limited inferential skills, and a lack of awareness of authorial bias. | Writing demonstrates lack of awareness of audience and does not fulfill writer's purpose; voice is inauthentic and/or inappropriate as demonstrated by tone, diction, and vocabulary. | Writing exhibits no central idea, or a disconnect between idea and supporting evidence, or insufficient supporting evidence. | Introduction, body, and/or conclusion are poorly focused or non-existent; ideas may be arranged illogically. | Writing demonstrates inappropriate use or lack of sources, awkward integration of researched materials, and/or incorrect or absent documentation. |
| **Practitioner** | Though competent, writing could improve from better application of one or two steps of the writing process. | Writing shows adequate comprehension and some inferential ability; writing shows an ability to engage with the text. | Writing demonstrates a basic awareness of audience and generally fulfills writer's purpose; tone, diction, and vocabulary are functional and appropriate. | Thesis is clear and substantially supported by evidence in a straightforward though perhaps mechanical way. | Writing shows a basic sense of beginning, middle, and end; a functional introduction, body, and conclusion; and, for the most part, focused and orderly paragraphs. | Most sources are appropriate and correctly documented. Research is sufficient to the assignment and adequately integrated. |
| **Expert** | Writing is polished and insightful, demonstrating a synthesis of the writing process. | Writing engages fully with the text, demonstrating developed inferential and evaluative skills. | Writing demonstrates a clear sense of audience and effectively fulfills the writer's purpose. Voice is distinctive; vocabulary is aptly chosen, lively, and sophisticated. | Thesis is clear, thought-provoking, and well focused, supported by vivid and concrete evidence. | Writing demonstrates a logical and clear structure, incorporating graceful transitions and unified paragraphs. | Primary and/or secondary sources are skillfully interwoven into the text to support the thesis. Research is thorough, and sources are correctly cited. |

# Course Descriptions

Below are brief catalog descriptions of the writing courses offered as part of the first-year writing program at BSC. Additional information about first and second year writing intensive seminars and upper-level writing courses offered by the English Department may be found in the *Bridgewater State College Undergraduate/Graduate Catalog*. Additional information concerning prerequisites and credits may be found there as well.

## ENGL 101: Writing I

The writer explores various techniques for discovering, developing and organizing ideas through intensive practice in composing short expository essays. Special attention will be given to mastering essential skills appropriate to academic writing.

## ENGL 102: Writing II

Continuing to develop essential skills, the writer learns and practices various techniques of argumentation. Special attention will be given to learning basic research skills and to integrating the ideas of others into one's own text. Emphasis is on longer and more substantive essays and a research paper.

There are also two variants of ENGL 101: Writing I designed to serve certain populations of students:

## Targeted ENGL 101: Writing I

The writer explores various techniques for discovering, developing and organizing ideas through intensive practice in composing short expository essays. Special attention will be given to mastering essential skills appropriate to academic writing with an emphasis on extra support for students given in the form of book clubs, consultations with a writing fellow, and additional advising sessions in the Academic Achievement Center.

# ENGL 101 XL: Writing for Non-Native English Speakers

The writer explores various techniques for discovering, developing and organizing ideas through intensive practice in composing short expository essays. Special attention will be given to mastering essential skills appropriate to academic writing with an emphasis on those areas that might prove difficult for students whose second language is English.

# Placement Procedures

The Academic Achievement Center uses various measures to ensure students that they are placed properly in one of the following four courses:

- Targeted ENGL 101: Writing I
- ENGL 101: Writing I
- ENGL 102: Writing II
- ENGL 101 XL: Writing for Non-Native English Speakers

While most students take two semesters of first-year writing, some students test directly into ENGL 102: Writing II.

Beginning first-year students are placed in writing courses via a faculty-scored writing sample administered at New Student Orientation. SAT-V scores are also a placement criterion for first-year students:

- SAT-V 500–590 automatically places a student in ENGL 101.
- SAT-V 600 or above automatically places a student in ENGL 102.

In addition, ACCUPLACER Reading + Sentence Skills tests are administered to non-degree, transfer or continuing students needing placement, and any first year students who missed the orientation writing sample opportunity. The combined Reading and Sentence Skills scores are yet another placement criterion for first-year students:

- Combined Reading + Sentence Skills scores below 153 automatically place a student in Targeted ENGL 101: Writing I.
- Combined Reading + Sentence Skills scores 153 and above place a student in ENGL 101: Writing I.

ACCUPLACER is not used for placement in ENGL 102: Writing II.

Non-native speakers are exempt from ENGL 101 XL if they have a TOEFL score of 550 or above, an ENGL 101 placement via ACCUPLACER, and a record of high school study of English.

# Transfer Students

Transfer students who have completed composition courses at other institutions should submit their transcripts to the Registrar's Office for evaluation.

Should the Registrar's Office not be able to make a determination, the student should fill out a Transfer of Credit form, attach a course description of the composition class taken at another institution, and submit it to the Humanities Office, 340 Tillinghast Hall. The Chair of the English Department will then determine if the course is the equivalent of either ENGL 101: Writing I or ENGL 102: Writing II.

# Course Management Information

## Attendance Policy

Each instructor of first-year writing will have an attendance policy stated on the syllabus. It is very important to be aware of this policy as excessive absences in most classes will result in a failure for the course or a lowered final grade.

## Grading Policy

Each instructor of first-year writing will have a grading policy that outlines the criteria for determining a final grade for the course. In addition, the policy will inform students if late work is accepted and, if so, if there is a penalty for late work.

## Midterm Progress Reports

At a determined time toward the middle of each semester, instructors are asked to submit warning grades for those students with a "D" or "F" grade. Instructors will notify students that these warning grades have been posted. In turn, students who receive such grades should set up an appointment with their instructors to discuss how more satisfactory progress can be achieved in the class.

## Withdrawals

In some cases, the instructor or student may deem it advisable for the student to withdraw from the course once a warning grade has been given. The deadlines for withdrawal from a course occur in the weeks following midterm progress reports. Specific dates are available online at www.bridgew.edu/Registrar/withdrawal.cfm. They are also available along with withdrawal forms from the Registrar's Office on the ground level of Boyden Hall.

# Incompletes

If a student wishes to apply to his or her instructor for a grade of IN (incomplete), this must be done in writing. Normally, incompletes are only given if circumstances beyond the control of the student occur after the official date for withdrawal from classes and if they impede completion of coursework by the end of the semester. Most of the coursework, however, should have already been completed. Both the instructor and student should agree on what remaining assignments must be completed, by when, and how these assignments will be collected and returned.

# How to Handle Emergencies

It is an unfortunate occurrence whenever a student receives a failing grade for a course—especially if the failure could have been avoided. Should an unexpected emergency occur during the course of the semester, such as a serious physical illness for the student or a family member, a severe emotional problem, or a critical financial problem, the student should immediately set up an appointment with the instructor. Failing that, the student should set up an appointment with the Chair of the English Department, whose office hours will be posted on the door of Tillinghast 339. Depending on the circumstance, to avoid failing the course, a student may be advised to take a medical withdrawal, a regular withdrawal, or an incomplete. Meeting with the instructor or department chair will be much more effective than later trying to hand in multiple assignments or to request an incomplete at the end of the course after having been absent from class for several weeks. *Last minute requests without prior notification of the instructor about the emergency situation usually result in a failure for the course.*

# Academic Integrity

Academic integrity refers to academic honesty—the avoidance of plagiarism or other forms of cheating. As stated in the *BSC Student Handbook*, "plagiarism and cheating are not condoned and are subject to academic penalty, which may result in a failure for the course in which the violation took place. A violation may result in a reduced grade, suspension, or dismissal from the college." (The entire policy can be found online at www.bridgew.edu/handbook/policiesprocedures/academicintegrity.htm.) The process is also detailed in the *Student Handbook*: the instructor, upon suspecting academic misconduct, has seven days to notify the student and meet to discuss the suspected infraction; the instructor then notifies the department chair and the associate vice president for academic affairs of both the infraction and the outcome of the meeting; in the case of repeat offenses, the student will go before the academic review panel. Students may also request that a case be brought before the academic review panel.

Instructors take cheating and plagiarism—the scholarly theft of words or ideas—very seriously. Most instructors will also see the handing in of the same paper to two teachers as cheating.

There are several things you can do to protect yourself from charges of academic misconduct. First, make sure you understand each instructor's definitions of cheating and plagiarism (which can shift slightly across the disciplines). If academic misconduct is not addressed on the instructor's syllabus or Blackboard course page, be sure to ask. Second, before handing in an essay, you can run it through TurnItIn.Com—a program available through Blackboard that will check for close paraphrases and un-cited quotes, as well as language used in other student essays. You can then use the results to further revise the paper. Third, be sure to keep all drafts of your work. Save your paper often, using separate files to save brainstorming notes, early drafts, middle drafts, later drafts, and the final draft (i.e. Draft.1, Draft.2, Draft.3). Then, if an instructor asks you if a paper has been plagiarized, you can show the instructor the paper trail, which details how your ideas and language have evolved. The paper trail may also indicate accidental plagiarism—forgotten citations, un-cited paraphrases, paraphrases that use language too similar to the source. Many instructors will be more forgiving of accidental plagiarism than intentional plagiarism, asking you to revise to correct citations, rather than giving a failing grade to the paper.

## Faculty Office Hours

All faculty members are expected to hold regular office hours and to post them on their office door and in their syllabi. Students should avail themselves of these hours if they need individual assistance.

## Class Cancellations

Information on the cancellation of individual class meetings by an instructor will be provided on the hotline telephone number 508-531-1391 after 7:00 a.m. Absences may also be viewed on the Web at www.bridgew.edu by clicking on General Links under BSC Students and then clicking on Faculty Absences. Cancellations due to inclement weather will be announced at telephone number 508-531-1777, which will provide a message only in the event of class delay or cancellation.

# Understanding a Course Syllabus

The course syllabi, which your college instructors pass out at the beginning of the semester, act as a contract between you and the instructor. Each syllabus provides information on the course goals, the instructor's expectations of the students for the semester, the kinds and dates of reading and writing assignments, and the formula by which the instructor will arrive at your final semester grade. Although individual syllabi may vary in the order in which this information is presented, they all provide this basic information for students.

Many instructors provide very detailed syllabi with additional information such as the nature of the learning styles applied in the course, the online materials students should have access to, and the date and time of the final examination. As you get your syllabi from instructors this semester, it is a good idea to go through them and underline or annotate information you know you will need.

In the following pages, a sample syllabus from ENGL 101 has been annotated to show you what information is present and how it might be useful to you. In these annotations, you can see how the information in the syllabus helps you understand the directions and expectations of the course.

It is also a good idea to create a calendar of due dates by placing the due date for each assignment on a master calendar, either in hardcopy or in the Calendar function in your BSC e-mail, Web Outlook. If you take time at the beginning of the semester to understand and collate the information from your course syllabi, you will save time later in the semester in planning your work. You will also avoid the embarrassment (and lowered grade) that results when you do not have an assignment completed on time.

A sample assignment calendar page can be found on the page immediately following the sample syllabus. At the end of this book, you'll find blank calendar pages for September 2007 through May 2008, which you can use to chart your own course assignments and due dates.

# A Sample Syllabus with Annotations

Each course you take in college will have a syllabus, which you can use to identify assignments in advance and to understand the course's goals, expectations, and evaluation measures. This sample syllabus is for an ENGL 101 class offered in Fall 2004.

**ENGL 101-05**
**3 credits; MWF at 10 a.m., Maxwell 309**
**Course Website on Blackboard**

**Instructor: Prof. Anne E. Doyle**

| | |
|---|---|
| Tillinghast #333 | Office Hrs: T, TH 9–10 |
| | and by appointment |
| A5doyle@bridgew.edu | Tel. and voicemail: 508-531-2886 |

**Course Objectives**: In this class, you will develop your knowledge in creating an argument and in the conventions of writing, as well as further developing your skills in the writing process and in critical thinking, reading, and writing. During the course of the semester, you will produce at least 20 pages of formal, revised text intended for an audience of college-educated readers. By the end of this class, if you have worked diligently on the course throughout the semester, you will:

- More effectively utilize a variety of essay organization strategies
- Apply advanced techniques of text coherence, including a variety of transitions and meta-statements
- More effectively use writing and reading for inquiry, learning and thinking
- Develop a vocabulary for talking about and improving your writing
- Evaluate others' work both in print and in multimedia sources
- Improve your command of sentence structure and build your vocabulary
- Develop flexible strategies for generating, revising, editing and proofreading texts

> **Comment:** Instructors usually place contact information (phone number, e-mail address, office hours) early in the syllabus. You should make a note of this information; it will allow you to contact your instructor with questions if necessary.

> **Comment:** Syllabi usually have a list of course goals. This information lets you know what sorts of knowledge or skills you should have by the end of the course. The course goals signal where the emphasis of the course will be placed. Thus, you can use these course goals as a filter to help you strategize what information will be most pertinent for you to use in studying for examinations and in preparing other kinds of course assignments.

**Teaching and Learning Methods:** This course will involve writing workshops, multiple drafts of required written products, and the active participation of class members in both large group and small group discussions. We will be making use of notebook computers (NCs), Web resources and our own Web course site in Blackboard. You will be expected to become familiar with Microsoft WORD, the campus word processing program, and with Microsoft Outlook, the campus email system—as well as Blackboard.

**Tips for Successful Learning in this Class:**

- Within the first week of this class, arrange to take the hour-long introductory classes offered free of charge to BSC students by the IT department regarding Outlook, WORD, and Blackboard.

- Expect your homework for this class to run 6–8 hours/week, and budget your time accordingly.

- Take *active notes* on your readings: make notes in the margins of the readings, and underline key ideas.

> **Comment:** Many instructors provide tips for success in the class. Information like this helps you plan your semester and determine how much time per week you'll need to devote to the various elements of the course.

- Never turn in a written text that you have not put aside for a day or two and then revised. Also, never turn in a text you have not proofread.

- Take advantage of my office hours, my email and voicemail: if you have a question about an assignment or about how you are doing, please ask.

- For help with your reading and with revision, use the Writing Center and the Reading and Study Skills Center (both located in the Academic Achievement Center in Maxwell Library, ground floor).

**Required Class Texts—Available in BSC Bookstore:**

Lunsford and Ruskiewiscz. *In the Presence of Others*
Diana Hacker. *A Writer's Reference*

In addition, you should have a good dictionary of your choice and two notebooks: one for class notes and one to use as a Reading Journal.

> **Comment:** The syllabus will always indicate which texts are required for the course. Under most circumstances, these texts will be available in the BSC Bookstore in East Campus Center.

**Assessments and Course Grades:** Your final grade in this class will be dependent on the following formula:

Quizzes . . . . . . . . . . . . . . . . . . . . . . . . . . . . . . . .10%

Summaries . . . . . . . . . . . . . . . . . . . . . . . . . . . . .10%

Workshops . . . . . . . . . . . . . . . . . . . . . . . . . . . .20%

Final Drafts . . . . . . . . . . . . . . . . . . . . . . . . . . .20%

Book Club Participation and Presentation
(includes Reading Journal) . . . . . . . . . . . . . .20%

Attendance/Participation . . . . . . . . . . . . . . . .20%

**Comment:** Sometimes called "Mechanics of the Course" or "Mechanics," this section of the syllabus lays out the formula by which the instructor will award final grades in the course. You should keep a close eye on your progress in the course; using the mechanics formula will help you see in advance what sort of grade you can expect in the class.

**Special Accommodations:** Any student who, due to a disability, needs special accommodations to participate in class and/or complete assignments must register with the Disabilities Resources Office in the Academic Achievement Center (Maxwell ground floor). The appropriate person at the AAC will provide a letter that the student must deliver to the instructor in person. If you need special accommodations, you should arrange for this letter and see the professor before the end of the DROP/ADD period so that reasonable accommodations can be made.

**Class Attendance:** The grade for class attendance and participation includes participation in class, participation in the weekly Book Clubs, AND participation in the mid-semester conferences you will have with your instructor. By "participation," I mean being ready for the activity as you enter the classroom, joining in discussions and offering your observations, promptly completing reading and writing assignments, and being fully engaged in the class's activities.

**Comment:** Most syllabi will indicate the instructor's attendance policy. NOTE: attendance is not the same as participation, so it is possible to attend every class session and still not get a high participation grade. But no one with many absences will be in a position to earn a high participation grade. Note, too, that many instructors have a limit on absences—after a certain number of absences or "unexcused" absences, the student can get a failing grade in the course.

This course *requires* your attention and attendance. Now, I realize emergencies occur—babies get sick, writers develop the flu, and car batteries die unexpectedly. Consequently, you have three "no-fault absence days," wherein you can phone or e-mail me *on or before your absence*, explain the situation and arrange to make up the class work with me. **No matter what the reason for a fourth absence, you will not be able to make up missing work done in class on any absence after your third absence;** consequently, your final grade will suffer. **And without evidence of a medical emergency,** *I will not accept ANY unexcused late work.*

**Vocabulary Quizzes:** We will have vocabulary quizzes every two weeks. Starting with September 8, I will expect you to be responsible for knowing any unfamiliar vocabulary words arising from our discussions of our class readings. The vocabulary quizzes will be held in Blackboard. For the definitions of the words from our common readings, we will depend on this URL: http://www.dictionary.com

**Other Quizzes:** Although I do not give surprise quizzes, I reserve the right to schedule additional reading quizzes (beyond those already in the syllabus) and quizzes on other class materials as seem appropriate. Each quiz will be announced both in class and in this course's Blackboard Announcements page at least 48 hours before it is given.

**Plagiarism:** Plagiarism occurs when a writer uses the idea(s) or language of another person without acknowledging the source. It is a grave crime in all colleges—one which can result in the plagiarist failing the course or being expelled from school. Plagiarism can be avoided through careful note-taking and the use of quotations marks and appropriate citation forms in writing.

To help you uncover any inadvertent plagiarism in your work, I will ask you to submit a penultimate draft through TurnItIn in our Blackboard site. You will be able to reach TurnItIn through Blackboard's Assignments page three days before the final draft is due. If the text is reported as having unacknowledged sources, you should immediately revise, acknowledge the sources, and then submit the paper through Blackboard's DropBox for the final grade.

> **Comment:** Many syllabi spell out the instructor's policy regarding plagiarism. At BSC, Academic Policies require that instructors forward the name of any plagiarist to the Provost's Office.

Plagiarized essays in this class will receive a grade of F. For further information on the English Department's plagiarism policy, please consult http://www.bridgew.edu/English/papers.cfm. A description of BSC's general plagiarism policy may be found on pp. 48-49 of the 2003-2004 *BSC Catalog*.

**Required Written Course Assignments:**

The written assignments are as follows:

- 2 content summaries of articles (written in class)
- 5 essay assignments, workshopped and revised
- other writing activities for the Book Club assignments
- a final, non-workshopped reflective essay
- a reading journal

**Style of Workshop Drafts and Final Drafts:** Your workshop and final drafts should be word-processed, with lines at 1½ space. The margins should be no more than 1 inch on the right and left; the first line of each paragraph should be indented. The font for essays should be size 11 or 12; you may NOT use Comic, Courier or Courier New fonts. Rather, choose a font like Times, Times New Roman, or even Arial. Each essay should be approximately 4–5 pages in length, and every source you've used must be acknowledged appropriately.

**Comment:** Most syllabi will stipulate the style and format of papers for the course. Failure to follow formatting or style requirements will result in a lower grade in most courses.

Should you miss a workshop during an excused or unexcused absence, you MUST make up that workshop by working with a tutor at the Writing Center, using the workshop form prepared by me for that assignment. You MAY NOT substitute an out of class-time workshop with a classmate, friend, or family member in place of this.

**Book Clubs:** In addition to the daily reading for this class, every class member will also be a member of a book club. These clubs will meet weekly throughout the semester to discuss a novel from among the five I've chosen. At the end of the semester, each book club will offer a 10-minute presentation on their book for the benefit of the rest of the class. It would make sense to have a brief synopsis of the book (no more than 2 minutes), followed by an analysis of the theme(s) your book club found most strongly present in the book. You might create and perform a debate between two or more key characters in the novel. Or you may create one or more monologues for the principal character(s). We will discuss the end-of-semester book club presentations in more detail at the mid-semester point, at which time I will have a handout for you on possible book club presentation activities.

**Reading Journals:** This assignment's intention is to help you keep track of and understand how you respond to your readings. Be sure to bring your reading journals to class on any day you are asked to do so. In particular, you must always have your reading journal with you the day of a book club meeting. In these journals, I will ask you to respond to some of the questions following the readings in *Presence of Others*. I will also ask you to respond to some questions regarding your book club novel. Finally, I'll provide a list of reading journal prompts you can use to help you keep track of your responses to readings for this class.

**Rationale for the Five Essay Assignments:** In ancient Greece, skilled rhetoricians (among them Plato and Aristotle) noted that we humans use argument as a means of reaching consensus as a community, as well as a means of publicizing and stabilizing that consensus. In other words, we humans use argument as a means to arrive at answers to questions like the following:

- Does a particular thing exist?   (Conjecture)
- If it does exist, what is it, or what is it like?   (Interpretation)
- Is it good or bad?   (Evaluation)
- What should we do about it?   (Proposal)

This way of thinking about kinds of argument (called *stasis* organization) is very useful for a writer. As soon as you decide what kind of argument you are making (Conjecture, Interpretation, Evaluation, or Proposal), you can begin to determine the kinds of argumentative structure and evidence you should use for the argument. For this class, we will be following the logic of *stasis* organization. During the course of the semester, we will write two different kinds of interpretations, two kinds of evaluations, and one proposal essay.

## Tentative Daily Schedule for Classes

### Week of Sept. 6: Getting Started

W   Introduction to the class; selection of books for book clubs; self-assessment

F   For this class, read pp. 1–14 in *The Presence of Others* (*Presence*). **Be prepared for a reading quiz on these pages**. Also, write a description of yourself as a reader, in response to "Examining Your Reading Habits," p. 5. Read, as well, pp. 3–12 in *A Writer's Reference* (*WR*) on planning a piece of writing. The first essay assignment will be handed out in class today. Begin keeping a reading log over this coming weekend.

### Week of Sept. 13: Interpretations—How Things Are

M   For today, read pp. 15–22 in *Presence* (a review of the writing process). **Be prepared for a reading quiz on these pages.** Also, for today, read pp. 13–16, on drafting an essay, in *WR*. Finally, read Dave Barry's "Guys Vs. Men," pp. 402–413 in *Presence*, paying attention to the marginal comments. In your reading log, respond to ex. 1 and 4.

W   Three hard copies (printouts) of your workshop draft of Essay 1 are due in class. For today, as well, read pp. 17–22 on revising, in *WR*.

> **Comment:** Syllabi will always have a section where daily reading and/or writing activities are spelled out. Looking ahead at the deadlines in the syllabus will allow you to plan your semester's activities. It is a good idea to note on your calendar the due dates for various activities in the class. That way, you will not be surprised by a due date you'd lost track of. **Following this sample syllabus, you will find an example of a calendar sheet with assignment due dates filled in, and following this example, you'll find several blank calendar sheets for your own use this semester.**

20

**F**      For today, read Mark Clayton's "A Whole Lot of Cheatin' Going On," in *Presence*, pp. 207–211. Respond to questions 1 and 3 in your reading journal. **Be prepared for a reading quiz on this essay.** Bring your notebook computers (NCs) to class today for in-class work.

## Week of Sept. 20: Interpretations—Definitions

NOTE: By the end of this week, students should have begun reading their novels for book club.

**M**      For today, read Stephen L. Carter's "The Rules about the Rules" in *Presence*, pp. 179–190, and respond to question 1 in your reading journal. Start keeping a record of all the times you hear or see the word "integrity" this week (Question 2, p. 189); we'll compare our results on Friday. **Be prepared for a reading quiz on the essay.**

**W**      Final draft of Essay 1 due in class. Also for today, read pp. 23–36, on paragraphs, in *WR*. Bring NCs to class for in-class writing.

**F**      **Vocab. Quiz 1 online in class today.** Today, too, bring in your collection of instances the word "integrity" was used this week. Bring your NCs to class with you today for the vocabulary quiz and for in-class work.

## Week of Sept. 27: Critical Definitions

**M**      For today, read David Brooks's "One Nation, Slightly Divisible" (in *Presence*, pp. 581–603. **Be prepared for a reading quiz on this essay.** Also, respond in your reading journal to questions 1 and 7.

**W**      For today, bring your NCs to class. We will do some preliminary work on Essay 2, which will be handed out in class today.

**F**      More work on our second essays in class. Bring your NCs.

## Week of Oct. 4: More on Critical Definitions

**M**      Workshop draft copies of Essay 2 (An Interpretation) due in class. Also for today, read pp. 37–43, on constructing reasonable arguments, in *WR*.

**W**      For today, read Neil Postman's "The Great Symbol Drain" in *Presence*, pp. 545–564. **Be prepared for a reading quiz on this essay**.

**F**      **Vocab. Quiz 2 online in class today.** Bring your NCs to class today for some in-class work. Also for today, read Barbara Kingsolver's "And Our Flag Was Still There," in *Presence*, pp. 604–612.

## Week of Oct. 11: A Look at Evaluation

**M**    **Columbus Day Holiday**

**W**    Final draft of Essay 2 due in class.

**F**    For today, read George W. Bush's "Speech to the Nation on Stem-Cell Research," pp. 353–358 in *Presence*. **Be prepared for a reading quiz on this essay.**

## Week of Oct. 18: More on Evaluation

**M**    For today, read Todd Oppenheimer's "The Computer Delusion," in *Presence*, pp. 298–328. **Be prepared for a reading quiz on this essay.**

**W**    Workshop draft copies of Essay 3 (An Evaluation) due online in Blackboard. Mid-semester conferences with Ms. Doyle begin today.

**F**    Online discussion group activities in Blackboard today. Mid-semester conferences continue.

## Week of Oct. 25: Mid-semester Evaluations

**M**    Online discussion group activities due today in Blackboard. **Vocab. Quiz 3 online today; check Announcements in Blackboard for location.** Mid-semester conferences continue.

**W**    Final draft of Essay 3 due online to Ms. Doyle via Blackboard. Mid-semester conferences continue.

**F**    For today, read "The Declaration of Independence" in *Presence*, pp. 517–521.

## Week of Nov. 1: More on Critical Evaluations

**M**    For today, read Douglass's "What to a Slave is the Fourth of July?" in *Presence*, pp. 522–535. Mid-semester conferences continue.

**W**    Essay 4 assignment handed out today. Bring your NCs to class today for work.

**F**    **Vocab. Quiz 4 online in class today.** Bring your introductions to Essay 4 to class today, along with your NCs.

## Week of Nov. 8: Relationship Between Evaluation and Proposal

**M**     Workshop draft copies of Essay 4 (An Evaluation) due in class.

      **No Wed. Classes: Thursday Schedule on Nov. 10**

**F**     For today, read Anthony Brandt's "Do Kids Need Religion?" (pp. 213–221 in *Presence*) and respond to questions 2 and 3 in your reading journal.

## Week of Nov. 15: Proposal Writing

**M**     Final draft of Essay 4 due in class. Also for today, read Robert D. King's "Should English Be the Law?" in *Presence*, pp. 428–440. **Be prepared for a reading quiz on this essay**.

**W**     Essay 5 assignment handed out today. Also for today, read pp. 46–54 in *WR* (on evaluating arguments).

**F**     **Vocab. Quiz 5 online in class today**. Also for today, read Ward Churchill's "Crimes Against Humanity," pp. 536–544 in *Presence*. Be prepared to discuss this essay in class, particularly in view of questions 1–3 and 8.

## Week of Nov. 22: More on Proposals

**M**     Bring your introduction and conclusion paragraphs to class today, along with your NC, for work in class.

**W**     Workshop draft copies of Essay 5 (A Proposal) due in class.

**Happy Thanksgiving! No Friday class this week.**

## Week of Nov. 29: Reflecting on Ourselves as Writers

**M**     Reading in *Presence* TBA.

**W**     Final draft of Essay 4 due in class. For today, read the Profiles of the Editors and Students Commentators" in *Presence*, pp. xxv–xxxiii. Be prepared to discuss which student editor's self-evaluation you preferred, and why.

**F**     **Vocab. Quiz 6 online in class today**. Beginning to prepare our final self-assessment: Essay 6.

## Week of Dec. 6: Book Clubs and Evaluating Ourselves

**M**  Book Club Panel Oral Presentation 1.

**W**  In-class work on our final self-assessments. Bring your NCs.

**F**  Book Club Panel Oral Presentation 2. Course Evaluation in class.

## Week of Dec. 13: More Book Clubs and Evalutating Ourselves

**M**  Final draft of Essay 6 due in class.  Book Club Panel Oral Presentation 3.

**W**  Last day of class. Vocab. Quiz 7 online in class today. Book Club Panel Oral Presentation 4.

Given the number of writing assignments in this class, there will be no separate final examination.

**Comment:** Many syllabi will indicate whether there will be a final examination and on what date the examination will occur. If there is no information about the examination date in the syllabus by the second half of the semester, you will find the information online at the BSC Homepage.

# Sample Assignment Calendar Page

| October 2004 — Assignments Due | | | | | | |
|---|---|---|---|---|---|---|
| **Sun** | Mon | **Tues** | **Wed** | **Thurs** | Fri | **Sat** |
| | | | | | 1<br>*Appmt.<br>Writ. Studio<br>tutor 1 pm<br>re: Essay 2* | 2 |
| 3 | 4<br>*Workshop<br>EN 101<br>Essay 2 in<br>class* | 5<br>*Math 101<br>Quiz* | 6 | 7 | 8<br>*EN 101<br>Vocal.<br>Q 2 online* | 9 |
| 10 | 11<br>*1st Phi.<br>2-page paper<br>due* | 12 | 13<br>*Final draft<br>EN 101<br>Essay 2* | 14 | 15<br>*EN 101<br>Reading Q<br>on Bush<br>speech* | 16 |
| 17 | 18<br>*EN 101<br>Reading Q<br>on<br>Oppenhein.<br>essay* | 19<br>*Math 101<br>Quiz* | 20<br>*Workshop<br>EN 101<br>Essay 3 in<br>Blackboard* | 21 | 22<br>*EN 101<br>Vocab. Q 3<br>online* | 23 |
| 24 | 25<br>*Meet CC<br>130 tutor<br>today in<br>Ac.Ach.Cen<br>11 am* | 26 | 27<br>*Final draft<br>En 101<br>Essay 3 due<br>to Dr. Doyle<br>Online* | 28<br>*History Test<br>today* | 29<br>*Midsem.<br>conf. with<br>Dr. Doyle in<br>Tilly 333,<br>9-9:30 am* | 30 |
| 31 | | | | | | |

# Student Resources

## Writing Studio

**Location: Academic Achievement Center, bottom floor of Maxwell Library**
**Phone: 531-2053**
**Website: Available on Blackboard (VC 305-001 Writing Studio)**

The writing studio offers free consultations to provide students and faculty feedback on their writing (or to brainstorm ideas to write about later). Writers come to the studio for feedback on many types of work, including the following:

- works to be submitted for publication
- papers written for classes
- creative writing such as fiction and poetry
- personal statements written for graduate school applications
- resumes and cover letters

In addition to individual consultations on any of these types of writing, the writing studio offers the following free services:

- **Standing appointments** for writers who would like the structure of meeting with a consultant at the same time every week.
- **A library of handouts** with helpful hints on how to write effectively. To access these handouts, visit our Blackboard website (VC 305-001 Writing Studio) or stop by the studio.
- **Links to several nationally-known online writing labs**, available on our Blackboard website (VC 305-001 Writing Studio).
- **A library of handbooks** describing conventions for grammar, mechanics, punctuation, syntax, and citation styles (available for use in the Academic Achievement Center; ask a consultant for help finding a handbook that meets your needs).

- **A library of books discussing how to write in a variety of disciplines** (located behind our desk, to be used in the Academic Achievement Center for two-hour periods).

- **Classroom visitations** in which a consultant visits a class for five or ten minutes to give an overview of the services we offer or to give a brief lesson on a topic of interest to the students and professor.

- **Writers' Café,** an opportunity for BSC students to read their work aloud to an audience of appreciative faculty, students, and parents. Students may read fiction, creative non-fiction, poetry, or academic work (including short research papers or excerpts of longer papers). The Writers' Café is held once each semester. Submissions may be turned in at the Writing Studio desk in the Academic Achievement Center (bottom floor of Maxwell Library) or emailed to writingstudio@bridgew.edul; be sure to include your email address and phone number.

## Making the Best Use of the Writing Studio

Here are some tips for making the best use of the Writing Studio:

- Bring your assignment sheet with you so that the consultant can see what criteria your professor will use to evaluate your work.

- Bring a print-out of your work; it's hard for consultants to give good feedback when reading on a computer screen. (If you don't have a print-out because you are at the brainstorming stage, that's fine.)

- Try not to wait until the day the paper is due to bring it to the studio. If you bring in your work several days *before* it's due, you'll have time to make substantive revisions rather than just a few random "quick fixes." In addition, any given consultation addresses only a limited number of issues, so consultants often recommend a follow-up appointment—something that you can't take advantage of when you bring in your work the day it is due.

- Bear in mind that the studio is a teaching unit, not a proofreading service. Writers who want feedback on grammar and punctuation can request that the consultant teach them how to find and correct these types of issues. Such work is a process rather than a quick fix and often requires a series of visits to the studio.

- Realize that the studio has a diverse staff of about 20 consultants. Feel free to work with different consultants until you find a good match for your specific needs as a writer.

# Academic Achievement Center

**Location: Bottom floor of Maxwell Library (by Starbucks)**
**Phone: 531-1214**

In addition to housing the writing studio, the Academic Achievement Center (AAC) houses the communication lab, content tutoring for GER and introductory courses, disability resources, English as a second language services, mathematics services, and study and research services. More information on each of these services is provided below.

## Communication Lab (531-2225)

- Assists students with topic selection, outline, research, and with presentation practice

## Content Tutoring for GER and Introductory Courses (531-1214)

- Supplements assistance provided by other AAC services through individual and group tutoring

## Disability Resources (531-1713)

- Ensures all individuals equal access to BSC programs and services
- Offers a number of services to students who have a documented medical condition, are physically challenged, or have emotional or learning disabilities

If you anticipate that you will need disability support services, please contact Disability Resources at (508) 531-1713, TTY (508) 531-6113, or FAX (508) 531-5240. Disability Resources will work with you to evaluate your needs, determine resource availability, and assist in coordinating accommodations.

## English as a Second Language Services (531-2805)

- Provides ESL tutoring and Conversation Partners for ESL students
- Provides ESL Assessment at Referral

## Mathematics Services (531-2013)

- Supports mastery of content in all mathematics courses

## Study and Research Services (531-2038)

- Teaches strategies for effective textbook study, note-taking, test-taking, and exam preparation
- Teaches effective research skills

# Counseling Center

**Location: Tillinghast 013 (In the hall between Health Services and the Mail Room) Phone: 531-1331**

Students may drop by or call the above number to make an appointment. Students visit the Counseling Center for many reasons, including the following:

- Feeling overwhelmed or stressed
- Concerns about relationships with friends, family, boyfriend/girlfriend
- A sense of sadness or hopelessness about a particular event
- Homesickness
- Feelings of anxiety, self-doubt, or depression
- Difficulty with motivation or procrastination
- Academic problems
- Difficulties with transitions
- Pregnancy concerns
- Difficulties with eating or sleeping
- Problems with alcohol or other drugs
- Eating disorders
- Rape, sexual assault, or relationship violence
- Suicidal thoughts
- Feeling that something is wrong and not being able to define it

The counseling center also offers couples counseling. In addition, online resources are available at www.bridgew.edu/CounselingCenter/. All counseling services at the Counseling Center are confidential.

# Library Information and Resources

Library Director: Michael Somers

## Library Hours during Semesters

| | |
|---|---|
| Sundays | noon to 11:45 p.m. |
| Mondays-Thursdays | 7:45 a.m. to 11:45 p.m. |
| Fridays | 7:45 a.m. to 5 p.m. |
| Saturdays | 8:30 a.m. to 4 p.m. |

Maxwell Library offers access to books, AV materials, periodicals and over 100 electronic databases. The Library building also houses classrooms, the offices of the Dean of Arts and Sciences, the Academic Achievement Center, a Testing Center, the Archives, a Technology Help Desk, and several academic departments.

The Library's "Ask a Librarian" service (http://www.bridgew.edu/Library/askalib.cfm) allows users to send reference and other questions even when the Library is closed, while the FAQ page (http://www.bridgew.edu/Library/faq.cfm) provides answers to the most commonly asked questions about the Library and its resources. The Library's main webpage (http://www.bridgew.edu/Library/index.cfm) offers a wealth of information about the library's resources and hours of operation as well as providing access to the electronic databases. In addition, Maxwell Library's most often-used forms are available online (http://www.bridgew.edu/Library/ddsfrm.cfm), including the InterLibrary Loan/Document Delivery Request Form, the Library Instruction Request Form, and the Reserve Request Form.

# Physical Layout

Maxwell Library's physical resources are described below.

## *Ground Floor*

Accessible from Park Avenue and the plaza between Maxwell and Rondileau Campus Center, as well as by stairway from the Library's First Floor. The following resources are available:

- Academic Achievement Center
- Classrooms
- Continuing Education Offices
- Library Lecture Hall
- Starbucks Coffee Bar
- Technology Help Desk

## *First Floor*

Accessible from Shaw Road and stairway from Ground Floor. The following resources are available:

- Circulation and Reserve Desk
- Computer Stations
- Copy Center and Printing
- Classrooms
- Dean and Associate Dean of Arts and Sciences
- Document Delivery Office
- Group Study Room
- Heritage Room
- Library Instruction Classroom
- Martha Denison Rondileau Room
- Microfilm Readers and Microfilm/Microfiche Collections
- Periodical Stacks
- Reference Desk
- Reference Stacks

*Second Floor*

Accessible by stairway and elevator. The following resources are available:

- Circulating Book Stacks
- Classrooms
- Communication Studies Department Offices
- Computer Stations
- Educational Resources Center
- Grants and Sponsored Research Offices
- Group Study Rooms
- Undergraduate Research Offices

*Third Floor*

Accessible by stairway and elevator. The following resources are available:

- Archives and Special Collections
- Circulating Book Stacks
- Classrooms
- Computer Stations
- Group Study Rooms
- Library Director's Office
- Lincoln Reading Room
- Music Department Offices
- Social Work Department Offices
- Technical Services

## Borrowing Books at Maxwell Library

To borrow books from the circulating stack, present the books and your CONNECT card to a librarian at the First Floor Circulation Desk.

**Reserve Books**

Books reserved for class use by instructors can be found at the Circulation Desk. You will be expected to present your CONNECT card.

## Circulating Videos

Maxwell Library has a large number of videos which can be checked out. After looking up the video in the Library's Webster Catalogue, go to the Circulation Desk on the first floor to ask for the video. You will be asked to present your CONNECT card.

## Online Research through Maxwell Library

Maxwell Library subscribes to a number of online databases, some of which carry full-text articles. Maxwell Library's databases may be accessed through the Library's Web-page (http://www.bridgew.edu/Library/index.cfm or http://www.bridgew.edu/Library), as can information on other Library services.

Information on research report formats like the **Chicago Manual of Style**, **APA** or **MLA** citation formats are available through the Library as well, at http://www.bridgew.edu/Library/styleman.cfm.

In addition, the Library has placed its entire catalogue of books online as **Webster**. You can access Webster both on-campus and off, by going to the Library home page at http://www.bridgew.edu/library, or by clicking on the Library link at the top of the BSC home page.

On campus, you have full access to Maxwell's databases for E-books (E-library), journal articles, and audio-visual materials—all of which are accessed through the Library home page. From off-campus, you must first click on "Use Library from Home" on the Library's homepage.

If you have any difficulties using the library's electronic resources from home, visit the Tech Help Desk in Maxwell Library or Moakley Hall.

## The Library Reference Desk

This desk is staffed by trained reference librarians who can help you as you search for materials. You can even make an individual appointment with the Reference Librarians to learn how to use the Library's many resources. Call the Reference Desk at 508-531-1394 to make an appointment.

## Scholarly Versus Unscholarly Research Resources

There are many different kinds of general-purpose information websites, like *AskJeeves.com*, *About.com* and *Wikipedia*. Such sources give the sort of information you might get about a subject from an encyclopedia. For the college writer, these general sources may function much the way an encyclopedia article can: they may provide you with the names of experts on the subject, standard definitions, and perhaps even the titles of useful articles. In other words, these resources best serve college writers not by becoming sources for the paper themselves, but by steering them to more scholarly or professional sources which will offer much more detailed information about the subject. Of course, Maxwell Library subscribes to one of the best general-information online encyclopedias, *Britannica Online*, which you can access through the Library's homepage.

Many college instructors specifically prohibit their students from using *Wikipedia*, *AskJeeves*, or other general Web sources as secondary sources for their research assignments. Many readers, too, regard these sources as unreliable, so using them can undermine your credibility. Before you settle for *Wikipedia* as an actual source for your research paper, check with the instructor about how acceptable this database is for citation in the assignment.

When a writing assignment calls for scholarly sources, you should look for materials which are written by scholarly experts in the field; have a lengthy list of references and refer to these sources in the text; and are published in scholarly venues—that is, in online or print journals which are carefully edited by a panel of scholarly editors. Generally, Google and similar Web tools do not distinguish scholarly from unscholarly sources, so carefully evaluate any materials you acquire through them

# Electronic Resources for Writing

## Notebooks and BSC's Wireless Campus

BSC is a "wireless" campus. All incoming freshmen are asked to purchase a notebook computer equipped with a wireless card. During the summer and the first weeks of the semester, BSC Tech Support works to provide each student's notebook computer with the codes with which it can access the campus wireless web. Although there are a few "dead spots" where the notebooks cannot make a wireless connection, the wireless web is easily available in most areas of campus, including the classrooms and most of the library.

Each summer, BSC's Tech Support publicizes the notebook requirements necessary for this wireless connection. Students and faculty seeking to purchase a compatible notebook system should look for the technical specifications posted as a link from the BSC homepage (http://www.bridgew.edu).

Students in ENGL 101: Writing I and ENGL 102: Writing II may be expected to bring their notebook computers to class. Check your instructor's syllabus for indications about where and when you should have your notebook computer handy.

As a matter of courtesy, if you choose to take your class notes on your notebook computer, you should ask your instructor if this is all right.

## Additional Computer Access at BSC

BSC maintains general access computer labs with desktop computers in Harrington Hall (Room 007), Rondileau Campus Center (ground floor), Conant Science Center (Room 201) and Moakley Center (Room 130). In addition, Maxwell Library has several computer pods on the first and second floor, as well as a few general access computers in the Academic Achievement Center on the library's ground floor. In addition, Honors Program students are invited to use the computers available in the Honors Program office in the Academic Achievement Center.

There are also Adaptive Computer Labs available for students needing adaptations of computer equipment. These can be found in Moakley Center (Room 130) and in the Academic Achievement Center (Maxwell 001).

With any campus computer, you will need to have activated your BSC User Account (see below) in order to access the programs and online services offered.

Whenever you use an open access lab computer—or any computer on campus—be sure to log off when you are done to avoid having someone else access your account and, perhaps, run up your printing bill.

## BSC's User Account and Outlook Webmail System

To take full advantage of the open access computers and many online services here at BSC—including the BSC Webmail—you must activate your **BSC User Account**. **Although you may have another e-mail address, you are expected to activate your BSC Webmail account and to use it for BSC business.** The college regularly sends messages to students via this system, and your English 101 instructor will expect you to use this system to send and receive course messages. Further, you *must* activate your BSC User Account in order to register for Blackboard, the BSC Course Management System (see below).

To register for your BSC User Account, you should have handy your social security number or your BSC Banner ID. To activate your BSC User Account, which provides access to BSC's Outlook for Webmail, go to the BSC homepage (http://www. bridgew.edu ) and scroll down the left-hand menu to **Account Registration**, at or near the bottom of this menu. Click on Account Registration and follow the onscreen instructions to claim and activate your BSC User Account to allow you to send and receive e-mail.

Note: You can access the BSC homepage from any computer that has Internet access, as well as from any of the InfoBear computers set up in many of the campus buildings. To access any additional information from InfoBear (like registration information or course grades), your BSC User Account must be activated

To reach your BSC e-mail account, you must go to the BSC homepage. Then in the left-hand menu, scroll down to Webmail Login, click, and use your BSC Username and password to log on. When you navigate away from your Webmail account, it will close.

# Blackboard Course Management System

Many courses at BSC make use of **Blackboard**, an online course management system which can be accessed both on and off campus through the BSC Webpage (http://www. bridgew.edu) or through BSC's Blackboard address (http://plato.bridgew.edu). You register for Blackboard in much the same way you register for your BSC User Account: go to the BSC homepage, go to Accounts Registration, and this time click on Blackboard Registration and follow the instructions there.

Should you have any questions about Blackboard or its use, check out the IT website *FAQs about Blackboard* at http://blackboard.bridgew.edu/student_help/bb_login.cfm.

# The W: Drive, Webpages, and On-Campus File Storage

BSC students have an automatic access to BSC's **W: drive (Webhost drive)**, where they can store files to use at any BSC machine or put up a personal webpage. To use the W: drive, you will need to map an on-campus computer to it at least once. Follow these instructions with your notebook computer or at another on-campus computer:

1. In the upper left corner of your computer screen, right click "My Computer."
2. Select "Map Network Drive."
3. From Map Network Drive screen, Select Drive "**W:**" from the drop down menu.
4. In the folder field type \\webhost\username. (Replace username with your BSC user name.)
5. Select Finish.
6. Double click "My Computer": you should see a "W" drive mapped to your webhost server.

If you have any questions about accessing the W: drive, check out http://it.bridgew.edu/CIS/WebDev/ConnectWebhost.cfm. If you would like to create your own personal webpage, go to the IT page devoted to this service (http://it.bridgew.edu/CIS/WebDev/Personal.cfm).

# Printing at BSC

Each BSC student is allocated $30 in free printing each semester. When a student prints in a classroom or lab on campus, the cost of printing is deducted from this free allocation. Black-and-white printing costs 10 cents per page ($0.10), and color printing costs 25 cents per page ($0.25). Students will see a notice on the computer screen each time they log on, informing them of the amount remaining on their account. If students exceed their free allocation, the cost of additional printing is added to their student bill at the same rates per page. To understand your rights and responsibilities regarding printing at BSC, see the IT page http://it.bridgew.edu/Support/StudentGuide/PAS/policy.cfm.

# Getting Help with Computer Problems

In addition to seeking help at the campus Technical Help Desks in Moakley 130 and in Maxwell Library (ground floor, near the elevators), you can also call the IT Help Desk at X 2555 (508-531-2555) or go online to IT Support Services at http://it.bridgew.edu/Support/.

# Places to Publish and Present

Sharing your work with a wider audience can be immensely gratifying. Not only is it a real pleasure to discover that readers outside of the classroom find value in your work, but the experience can add to your confidence as a writer, empowering you to continue writing and seeking wider audiences. Bridgewater State College offers a wealth of venues for sharing your writing with a wider audience, both in print and through public readings. Below, we have listed a number of venues that accept work from first-year students, but as you continue through your college career, you will discover even more venues, such as newsletters, journals, and conferences dedicated to specific majors.

## Student Publication Venues

### *thebridge*

*thebridge*, BSC's student-run literature and fine arts journal, is an annual volume of student fiction, creative non-fiction, poetry and visual art. Each year since its inception, *thebridge* has won prestigious awards from the Columbia Scholastic Press Association. Submissions are accepted between the end of April and the last day of fall semester. For details about the submission process, and to view past volumes of *thebridge*, go to <http://thebridgejournal.com/index.html>.

### *The Comment*

*The Comment*, BSC's student-run newspaper, encourages students unaffiliated with the newspaper to submit editorials and articles. You can submit letters to the editor to <www.bridgew.edu/SGA/TellTheComment.htm>. To submit an article, contact the managing editor at 508-531-1719 or drop by the newspaper's office in Campus Center 103. You may also be interested in applying for a staff position; you can apply online in late spring or early fall at <www.bridgew.edu/SGA/comment.htm#Staff>.

## Embracing Writing

*Embracing Writing*, the volume you are currently reading, publishes student work written in ENGL 101 and 102. Awards are given for excellence in the following categories: Expository or Persuasive Writing, Creative Non-Fiction, Researched Writing, and Revision. Winners receive $50 and guaranteed publication in the next edition of *Embracing Writing*. For more information about the submission process, please see the entry form in the back of this book. This form is available electronically at <www.bridgew.edu/wac/WritingAtBSC/StudentPublicationVenues.cfm>. If you have any questions, contact Dr. Anne Doyle, the Writing Program Administrator, at 508-531-2886 or a5doyle@bridgew.edu.

## The Undergraduate Review

*The Undergraduate Review*, administered by the Adrian Tinsley Program for Undergraduate Research, publishes student research and creative work done as part of a class or under the mentorship of BSC faculty. Published annually, this journal features work from students across the college and has space set aside for work from first-year students. For details about the submission process and deadlines, go to <www.bridgew.edu/ATP/ur.cfm>.

# Student Presentation Venues

## Midyear Symposium of First and Second Year Student Work

Sponsored by the Office of Undergraduate Research, the Midyear Symposium features work by first and second year students. This event, to be held on December 12, the last day of classes for fall semester, is open to both creative and research projects, and both oral and poster presentations are welcomed. To see what past years' participants have done, go to <www.bridgew.edu/OUR/midyearsymposium.cfm>. If you are interested in presenting at the symposium, you should talk to the instructor of the course for which you did the work you want to present. More information will be available on the OUR website.

## Undergraduate Research Symposium

Sponsored by the Adrian Tinsley Program and the Office of Undergraduate Research, the Undergraduate Research Symposium features both research and creative work by students from across the college. The Symposium is held at the end of April in the spring semester. All BSC undergraduate students, regardless of major or year, are encouraged to participate, and faculty are welcome to invite their classes to attend all or part of the Symposium. For more information about the proposal process and the event, go to <www.bridgew.edu/ATP/symposiumgeninfo.cfm>.

## The Writer's Café

Sponsored by the Writing Studio and the Academic Achievement Center, The Writer's Café provides a forum for you to read your work aloud to an appreciative audience. You may submit fiction, creative non-fiction, poetry, or academic work, including short research papers or excepts of longer papers. You may submit multiple pieces, and you may submit work every semester. Note that many writers who read at The Writer's Café go on to become consultants in the Writing Studio. The Writer's Café is held once each semester. In the fall, The Writer's Café will be held Monday, November 19th; the deadline for submissions will be Monday, November 5th. In the spring, The Writer's Café will be held Monday, April 14th; submissions are due by Monday, March 31. Submissions can be emailed to writingstudio@bridgew.edu. Please be sure to include your phone number along with your submission.

## National Conference on Undergraduate Research (NCUR)

Since its inception in 1987, NCUR has become a major annual event drawing over 2,500 undergraduates, faculty, and administrators from over 300 colleges and universities across the country to present, hear, and discuss undergraduate creative and scholarly work. Each year, a number of BSC undergraduate proposals are accepted. To simplify travel and reduce costs, the group travels together to NCUR, which was held this past year in the San Francisco Bay area. For more information, go to <www.bridgew.edu/ATP/ncur.cfm>. While it is not often that first year work is accepted for presentation at this conference, this event is still good to keep in mind as you continue with your academic career.

# Helpful Strategies for Writing

Note: Each future edition of *Embracing Writing* will feature an additional strategy for writing well.

## Revision in First-Year Writing Courses

ENGL 101: Writing I and ENGL 102: Writing II are writing-intensive courses. Your instructors for these courses will expect you to revise the formal writing you do. To help you with this revision, you may be asked to participate in peer review workshops, small group conferencing, or conferences with the instructor. In all cases, you should revise the draft before bringing it in for analysis by peers or the teacher. Never bring an unrevised draft forward for critiquing; you are wasting your time and the time of your readers. Rather, do the best revision you can with the writing you will workshop or conference on with others. Then, after getting feedback from the reader or readers, carefully revise your work again.

Revisions involve four possible activities: you can **add** text, **delete** text, **move** text from one area to another, or **substitute** one portion of text for another. When you revise, remember that you are in the process of re-thinking your text. You can make substantive, major changes to your writing, as well as smaller changes.

When you revise a paper, your revision will be more effective if you revise your work on three levels: high order, mid-order, and low-order. **High-order revisions** are those that change the logical flow, focus, or overall structure of the paper. In high-order revision, you might change your thesis, add or subtract supporting claims or materials, re-order the paper's structure, or substitute ideas. After high-order revision, you should focus on **mid-order revisions**. In mid-order revisions, the writer focuses on paragraph-level issues. Here too, you might substitute ideas, add or subtract sentences, or reorder sentences. After mid-order revisions, you should turn your attention to **low-order revisions**, which are sentence-based. Here, the writer is concerned with sentence structure, spelling, mechanics (including punctuation), and word choice. Again, you might add or subtract words from the sentence, substitute words or punctuation, or reorder the sentence's structure.

You'll find that if you focus on all three levels of revision (instead of just one or two), and if you approach the revisions working from high, to middle, then to low-order, your final draft will be a much more effective piece of writing. This approach to revision (higher-to-lower-order focus as well as repeated passes at revision) makes sense because a change at one of the higher levels of the draft can really affect the nature of the paragraphs and the sentences; in addition, each revision serves to strengthen the overall writing.

# Playing with Revision

Michelle Cox and Katherine E. Tirabassi

*You need to get some writing down on paper and to keep it there long enough so that you can give yourself the treat of rewriting. What you need is a ballpoint pen so that you can't erase and some cheap paper so you can deliberately use a lot of it . . . Where are your notes to yourself? Where are your lists? . . . Where are your quoted passages? Where is your chaos? Nothing comes of nothing!*

Ann Berthoff, "Recognition, Representation and Revision"

Revision is the time when you are free to play with language, experiment with form and voice, and explore your ideas and memories more deeply. The following prompts were developed to help guide you in revision, providing multiple ideas for further developing content, organization, and style.

The prompts listed under "Developing the Meaning" and "Style and Eloquence" are useful when revising a wide range of texts, from researched essays, to letters to the editor, to creative non-fiction. You may find the prompts listed under "Playing with Time" and "Layering in the Details" most useful when revising works of creative nonfiction.

## Developing the Meaning

1. **Finding the Focus**: Does your essay feel unwieldly, scattered? Read through the essay and circle the part that most clearly zones in on what you want to write about or hints at an insight you experienced while writing. In the rest of the piece, underline the phrases that need to be in the next draft. Now, rewrite, starting as close to the circled part as you can, and ending soon after the circled part ends. You may find that this new writing leads to a whole new draft, or you may choose to incorporate this writing into your existing draft.

2. **Do You Really Mean It?** Revision gives the opportunity to reflect on and further develop your ideas. Read over your draft, and ask yourself if you still

believe or agree with everything you wrote. Write reflective notes in the margins as you read, and then revise, while referring to these notes.

3. **Talk about Your Writing**: Ask someone to read your writing who is willing to talk with you seriously about what you've written. During this conversation, note what your reader asks questions about, finds interesting, wants to know more about. When you revise, picture this reader as your audience.

4. **Looping:** Look through your draft and identify a line that calls out to you, one that seems to hold meaning. Take out a new piece of paper, copy this line at the top, and freewrite from it, pushing to further develop meaning as you go. Look over this new writing, identify another line that calls out to you, and repeat the process.

## Style and Eloquence

5. **Activate Your Verbs**: There are going to be situations when passive voice is preferable, such as when you are writing for scientific audiences or in cases when you want to deemphasize the subject. However, active verbs are often more direct than passive verbs. A test you can use to distinguish between active and passive voice is to try adding a "by . . ." phrase to the sentence. If you can add a "by . . ." phrase, the sentence uses passive voice. For example: Active: *Karen made the cookies.* Passive: *The cookies were made by Karen.* The second example is passive, because a "by . . ." phrase is added: *The cookies were made by Karen.* One more tip: Using too many "ing" verbs can slow down the pace of your prose. For example, instead of *I was running*, use *I ran*. Save "ing" verbs for times when you want to slow the action in a scene, such as describing the moment before an accident occurred or watching a leaf falling to the ground.

6. **Cut, Cut, Cut**: Comb through your essay and cut as much as you possibly can. Try for fifteen words per page. Cut extra words that don't add meaning, such as "really," "very," "basically," "thing," "it," "it was," "it is," "there were," "there is," "this is," and "that." Example: *My brother's constant whining is one of those many characteristics that really frustrates me to no end* can be cut to *My brother's constant whining frustrates me*. Cut wordy phrases that don't add meaning, such as *on the other hand, due to the fact that, needless to say, in my personal opinion, at this point in time*. Cut redundant words, such as "big tall skyscraper." The words "big" and "tall" have similar meanings, and using the specific word "skyscraper" tells your reader that the building you're referring to is a large building.

7. **Sentence Variety**: Readers appreciate a change of pace, and varying sentence lengths and structure can add that sense of texture to your writing, and help

you better emphasize key pieces of information. Comb through your draft and focus in on your sentences. Count the number of words in each sentence. How many sentences are the same length? Look at the structure of your sentences. How many include introductory phrases, conjunctions, or dependant clauses? Read your essay out loud, listening to the rhythm, noting places where you stumble over a word or strive to emphasize something that's not being emphasized by the writing. Then revise, using short sentences for emphasis, long sentences for depth and description, moving important pieces of information to the ends of sentences for added emphasis.

8. **Focusing on Pronouns**: Here are some strategies for tightening your writing in relation to pronoun use: Comb through your draft and circle all instances of "it." The phrase "it is" at the beginning of a sentence (*It is a quiet, gentle rain*) can be used for emphasis, but overuse waters down this emphasis. Other uses of "it" can make writing sound vague. "There" at the beginning of the sentence can have the same effect. Try replacing "it" and "there" with more specific words. Now circle all uses of the words "this" and "these." Many times, when "this" or "these" is not followed by the word the pronoun is referring to, the writing can sound vague and foggy (e.g., *This is long and cumbersome* versus *This sentence is long and cumbersome*). Then, circle all uses of he, she, you, we, they, etc. Make sure each pronoun has a clear referent, a particular person that the pronoun refers to.

## Playing with Time

9. **Flashback**: Narratives don't need to follow a strict timeline starting at the beginning and detailing each chronological event to the end. In fact, doing so can drag out your story, compelling you to include details and events that are not essential to your main point. Try mixing it up by using a strategy like flashback, which allows you to move back and forth in time and only include the details and events that are significant. One thing to watch out for: make sure you make the shift in time clear to your reader, using signals such as changes in verb tense (present tense to past tense), white space surrounding the flashback, and the return to specific details that ground the reader in the framing story.

10. **Time Stretch**: Psychological time operates very differently from clock time. Sometimes an incident that only took a few minutes holds a great deal of significance. Look for an incident like this in your narrative, and write a page or more about it. Recall those few minutes in detail. Replay them in slow motion. Try to use at least three of the five senses.

11. **Time Summary**: Time summaries are useful when you want to indicate to the reader quickly that a long period of time has passed or to indicate the repetition and similarity of events, such as when you want to describe a typical day at the office or what usually happens at family reunions. To use this technique, compress a long period of time into a paragraph. Let readers know the length of time you are summarizing. Words like "often," "frequently," "always," "usually," "again and again," "sometimes," and especially "would" suggest that actions are repeated. Here's an example of a time summary: *Summers at the Cape always started like this. The long wait to cross the Bourne Bridge, while my sister and I talked about all that we would do that summer in Sandwich. The thrill of unlocking the cottage door and running through the rooms, making sure nothing had changed. The rush of visiting our favorite haunts again—the Boardwalk, Pizzas by Evan, Mary's Bookstore. But then reality would set in Monday morning when Dad left to work in Worcester for the week, and we'd remember the long weeks of boredom, without Dad, without familiar neighbors, without friends from school.*

## Layering in the Details

12. **Describe a Person**: Choose a person relevant to your essay's focus and describe all physical features, dress, smell, mannerisms, how he/she talks, how he/she interacts with people, so that your reader would be able to identify this person in a crowded room.

13. **Describe a Place**: Fully describe a specific location relevant to your essay's focus. Describe everything you see, smell, hear, taste, feel. Bring the reader right into your experience of this place.

14. **Describe an Object**: Choose a significant object that you mention in your essay, and fully describe it, referring to all of your senses. For example, if you mention a journal, show the cracks in the journal binding, the frayed edges of the fabric, the way your handwriting looks messy and excited at some places, and relaxed and contemplative in other places.

15. **Take Another Look**: Return to a place or dig out an object that you mention in your essay. Write about new details that you notice or new memories that arise.

16. **Talk to Someone Who Knows**: Informally interview a person who is important to the events you discuss in one of your pieces. Ask this person questions to fill gaps in your memory. Insert what you learn into your essay.

17. **Unbury a Story**: Find a line in your essay that seems to hide a story, and unbury that story. You might find a line that "tells" but doesn't "show." Open up that story. Belief statements, such as "I can't write," often hold one or more stories within them. Choose one of these stories to tell.

18. **Add, Add, Add**: Comb through your essay and add details that help your audience better understand what you see and mean when you use certain words. Change vague nouns (*car*) to specific nouns (*Nissan Quest*), general adjectives (*red*) to specific ones (*metallic cherry*), direct statements (*my minivan handles well*) to metaphors (*When shifting across three lanes to get to my exit, my minivan handles like what I imagine a racecar to feel like, hugging the road while cleanly gliding to the next lane, and responding quickly to my every move*).

Prompts #5, 6, 7, 9, 10, 11 are inspired by Rebecca Rule and Susan Wheeler's *True Stories: Guides for Writing from Your Life*. Porsmouth, NH: Heinemann, 2000.

# The "Break-It-Down" Approach
## How to Make your Writing Reflect your True Intelligence

Dr. Kathryn Evans
Director, BSC Writing Studio

Many students finish writing a paper, read it over once, and print it out for submission. Unfortunately, this process can result in writing that does not reflect your true intelligence, because if you're like most writers, reading your work only once doesn't allow you to notice all the glitches that plague even the best writers' early drafts. Almost all writers—including professional writers—overlook problems and miss opportunities to strengthen their writing any given time they re-read their work. This is simply the limitation of the human brain; we're very smart, but we can only do so much at once.

To produce writing that reflects your true intelligence, try to avoid reading your paper only once before submitting it. Instead, consider a "break-it-down" approach in which you *read your document one time for each area in which you are developing as a writer.* One writer, for instance, might read her work once to see if it's focused, another time to see if she has enough evidence to support her claims, and still another time to look for comma splices. Another writer might read his work once for organization, once for transitions, and once for fragments.

Most writers find that this "break-it-down" strategy works far better if they print out their work rather than reading it on a computer screen. Because print-outs have a higher resolution, they are quicker and easier to read. In addition, printing out your paper allows you to spread out your pages and see all your work at once rather than one screen at a time, thus enabling you to look for big-picture patterns (e.g., body paragraphs that don't quite follow through on your thesis, transitions that don't quite tie one paragraph to the next, etc.).

After you print out your work, read it one time for each issue you want to work on. In collaboration with a reader such as a classmate, professor, or writing studio consultant, use the space below to outline the issues to consider each time you read your paper.

Personalized List of Issues:

- _____

- _____

- _____

- _____

Reading your work one time for each of these issues can lead to significant improvements in your writing—not only in "big-picture" issues such as focus and support but also in the grammatical issues that can so deeply undermine a writer's credibility. *Many writers have found this "break-it-down" approach to be the single most important set of steps they have taken in becoming more effective writers.*

# Transitions, Cohesion and Coherence

One approach that helps with middle- and lower-order revision is to consider how your paragraphs' sentences relate to each other—that is, how the text transitions from paragraph to paragraph and from sentence to sentence. Transitional words and phrases, cohesion, and coherence all help the readers follow the text you are writing. **Cohesion** refers to the way each sentence of a text is understood to be related to the previous sentence; **coherence** refers to the fact that a well-structured text allows the reader to form a mental picture of the whole text's point or idea. Coherence is not possible without cohesion.

## Transitions

Transitional words and phrases (*in addition, thus, therefore, moreover, nonetheless, nevertheless, in comparison, dissimilarly, consequently,* etc.) contribute greatly to the cohesion of a piece of writing. The transitions you use act as signposts for your readers, helping them understand how the sentence they are reading is logically related to what has already been stated. Beyond using transitional phrases, you can use other cohesive techniques like given and new information and repetition and substitution of key terms to help your readers form a coherent sense of your text and follow what you are saying.

## Given and New Information

A text is often more cohesive when, after its first sentence, all its subsequent sentences refer to ideas that previous sentences have stated or implied. Readers expect that after the first sentence of a text, *each subsequent sentence will begin with given information* (something already mentioned or alluded to) *before adding new information in the second part of the sentence.* A piece of writing that follows these expectations regarding given and new information is likely to be clearer and easier to read.

Read the following paragraphs and determine which seems easier to read. In the first one, the writer wrote without considering the flow of given and new information; in the second one, the writer revised the paragraph to exploit the flow of given and new information. In each paragraph, the given information is **bolded** and the new information is underlined.

*First Draft—Doesn't Consider Given and New Relationships*

When Reagan assumed the presidency, he wanted to succeed at two major goals: reaffirming America as a military superpower and restoring the health of the American economy. <u>The drop in unemployment figures and inflation and the increase in the GNP testify to</u> **his success in the second goal.** <u>Our increased exposure to international conflict without any clear set of political goals indicates</u> **less success with the first**.

*Revision—Exploits Given and New Relationships*

When Reagan assumed the presidency, he wanted to succeed at two major goals: reaffirming America as a military superpower and restoring the health of the American economy. **He was indeed successful in his second goal of restoring the economy,** <u>as testified by the increase in the GNP and the drop in unemployment and inflation.</u> **He was, however, less successful in his first goal of reaffirming America as a military superpower**, <u>as indicated by our increased exposure to international conflict without any clear set of political goals.</u>

Readers usually find it easier to read a text when most of its sentences put given information before new information.

## Repetition and Substitution of Key Terms

To avoid sounding repetitive, writers often substitute words with their synonyms. This can relieve monotony, as can the use of varied sentence lengths and structures. However, it can be very effective and supportive of cohesion and coherence to repeat the key term of your argument, rather than use a multitude of synonyms. As you revise your writing, ask yourself in each case whether it is better to use a key term in a particular sentence, or whether your readers will be able to understand a synonym substitute for this term.

In the next few pages, we see one writer's movement through revision to a polished and effective final draft.

# Thank You Letter to Interviewer

Revisions by Bryan Candito

*The different versions of this letter, written to thank an expert Candito had interviewed as a source to cite in a paper, illustrate the meaning of "revisions": literally, "to re-see" in Latin. Rather than making minor editing changes in each draft, Candito adds substantially more evidence to support his implicit claim that his interviewee's time was well-spent.*

*In the process of making these substantive changes, Candito relied on two important strategies—strategies that will also serve you well. First, he revised on his own; he read his first draft and came up with his own ideas about how his second draft could be better. His third draft is based on feedback from his classmates, and his final draft, on feedback from his professor. While not all students will choose to revise a document so many times, doing this many rounds of revision will help you produce the work that you are capable of.*

*To get a sense of just how big a difference revision can make, you might want to compare the effectiveness of Candito's first and last drafts in terms of how well they fulfilled his goal: persuading the reader that the time he spent being interviewed by Candito was indeed helpful. Would you say that the last draft is moderately or significantly more successful than the first?*

24 Fisher Rd.
South Weymouth, MA. 02190
April 12, 2007

Mr. Keys
Acting Proffessor
Bridgewater State College
XXX Summer St.
Bridgewater, MA XXXXX

Dear Mr. Keys,

I would like to take some time to thank you for taking the time out of your busy schedule to talk to me about writing a screen play. Your explanation of what makes a good screenplay will be extreemly helpful for me when I am writing my paper.

The website you told me about where I am able to acces actual movie scripts has proven to be invaluable. ~~My search had been~~ unsucessfully to find the standard format for a screenplay. ~~~~ My search to find the proper format of a screen play had been unsuccessful and may have remained that way without your help.

54

24 Fisher Rd.
South Weymouth, MA 02190
April 12, 2007

Mr. Keys
Acting Professor
Bridgewater State College
123 Summer St.
Bridgewater, MA 02325

Dear Mr. Keys,

I would like to take some time to thank you for taking the time out of your busy schedule to talk to me about writing a screenplay. Your explanation of what makes a good screenplay will be extremely helpful for me when I am writing my paper.

*informed me of*

The website you ~~told me about~~ where I am able to access actual movie scripts has proven to be invaluable. My search to find the proper format of a screenplay had been unsuccessful (and may have remained that way without your help). Your insight on the elements of a storyline was equally (helpful) → *synonym* Until you told me, I had never really noticed that the main conflict of the story always occurs within the first 12 minutes. This information has given me the insight that I needed to understand writing a screenplay.

*have provided me with*

Thank you again for your time; the information you (have given me) will allow me to write a successful analysis of the screenplay genre.

Sincerely,

Bryan Candito

___

**strengths**
1) good syntax (e.g. "invaluable")
2) good detail
3) correct format

**things to consider**
1) 1st paragraph, maybe talk about how much knowledge you gained
2) write about how you both share the same interest in movies (screenplays?)
3) avoid repetition

24 Fisher Rd.
South Weymouth, MA 02190
April 12, 2007

Professor Thomas Kee
Acting Department
Bridgewater State College
123 Summer St.
Bridgewater, MA 02325


Dear Professor Kee,


I would like to take some time to thank you for ~~providing me with an appointment to~~ talking to ~~you~~ me about the screenplay genera despite your ~~having such a very~~ busy schedule. Your explanation of what makes a good screenplay will be extremely helpful for me when I am writing my paper.

The website you informed me of where I was able to access actual movie scripts has proven to be invaluable. My search to find the proper format of a screenplay had been unsuccessful (and may have remained that way without your help). Your insight into the elements of an effective storyline was equally handy. Until you told me, I had never really noticed that the main conflict of the story or "inciting incident" as you called it, always occurs within the first 12 minutes. Also, I appreciate how you helped me understand the importance of focus in screenplay writing. Knowing that all of the conflicts that occur in the screenplay should bring the main character of the film either closer to or further away from resolving the conflict established in the inciting incident is a very convenient way for me to distinguish between effective and ineffective screenplays. This information has given me the insight that I needed to understand the screenplay genera to a much greater extent.

Thank you again for your time; the information you have provided me with will allow me to write a much more successful analysis of the screenplay genre than I could have even dreamed of writing without your help.


Sincerely,

Bryan Candito

24 Fisher Road
South Weymouth, MA 02190
April 12, 3007


Professor Thomas Kee
Theater Department
Bridgewater State College
19 Park Avenue
Bridgewater, MA 02325


Dear Professor Kee,

I would like to take some time to thank you for talking to me about the screenplay genre despite your busy schedule. Your explanation of what makes a good screenplay will be extremely helpful for me when I am writing my paper.

The website you informed me of where I was able to access actual movie scripts has proven to be invaluable. My search to find the proper format of a screenplay had been unsuccessful (and may have remained that way without your help). Your insight into the elements of an effective storyline was equally handy. Until you told me, I had never really noticed that the main conflict of the story, or "inciting incident" as you called it, always occurs within the first 12 minutes. Also, I appreciate how you helped me understand the importance of focus in screenplay writing. Knowing that all of the conflicts that occur in the screenplay should bring the main character of the film either closer to or further away from resolving the conflict established in the inciting incident is a very convenient way for me to distinguish between effective and ineffective screenplays. This information has given me the insight that I needed to understand the screenplay genre to a much greater extent.

Thank you again for your time; the information you have provided me with will allow me to write a much more successful analysis of the screenplay genre than I could have even dreamed of writing without your help.

Sincerely,


Bryan Candito

# Sample Essays

To give you a sense of the kinds of writing being produced in ENGL 101 and ENGL 102, *Embracing Writing* includes a number of sample essays by students at Bridgewater State College.

In this issue, we have provided examples of creative non-fiction/personal essays and researched writing. In each case, one of each type has been annotated to illustrate strategies that you may find useful in your own writing.

Amy Peterson

# Fine Lines

How it all began I'm not too sure. It always becomes a haze once the madness sets in. Everything tends to come back in bits and pieces, just a series of chronological facts that don't mean a thing separately. I can recall pressure. A tight knot forming in my chest. It starts in my throat and spreads, cancerous, until I can't breathe. I'm Alice down the rabbit hole and I can't quite find the right cake to eat and suddenly everything is tiny. I'm too big for the space I'm in, and the doorway to the outside definitely can't accommodate me. There is not enough space or oxygen in the entire atmosphere to make me feel calm. I hear this is called a panic attack. What it's called is irrelevant though; when it takes over the last thing you're concerned with is what it's called.

Some people think this kind of thing just happens. That there's just a psychotic break and someone just loses it. When you're in it though, time slows down. The actual act that is perceived as "crazy" isn't the worst part; it's the agonizingly drawn-out loss of total control. It's the feeling of climbing an immense and wobbly ladder when you're terrified of heights, and the whole contraption teeters on the edge of oblivion. Anticipation always feels worse than the actual fall.

I don't take the stairs. I can't trust my shaky legs to make it the whole way down in one piece. So I sit in the elevator and compose myself. At the bottom I calmly cross the road to some gas station, your typical Cumberland Farms type set up. The frigid wind at my back almost wills me through the door. It was a simple transaction: find package of razors, give the cashier money, walk away. He smiles at me as he slides me my change.

**Comment [S1]:** This is an excellent title for a piece of creative non-fiction. It suggests the focus of the essay, and it has a double meaning that becomes apparent after one reads the essay—a double meaning that emphasizes the complexity of the writer's point.

**[Comment [S2]:** Works of creative non-fiction often begin *in medias res*, a Latin phrase meaning "into the middle of things." In this opening sentence, for instance, we're not sure what "it" refers to. While readers of an academic essay would likely be disoriented by an *in medias res* beginning, in this genre such beginnings can work well to draw readers in.

I grin back. How ironic. After all, facades are always better when they're nice pretty ones.

Finding an empty stall was easy. Everyone was away at dinner except for my roommates. Somehow I get an individual blade out of the unassuming white case. I place it against my forearm. Moments later a wet, scarlet line appears. It's funny how people assume this hurts because I never feel a thing. Nothing resembling pain anyway. The pressure lifts and a peaceful deep breath refills my lungs. The ladder finally tips and I can float with no thought of hitting bottom.

As sick as this may seem, that red line is one I walk all the time. It is the thin line between who I am and who I should be. It feels like zero gravity, the sweet madness that washes over you when you let go.

All better.

**Comment [S3]:** Note that in creative non-fiction, unlike academic writing, fragments are considered acceptable. In this paragraph, the fragment "How ironic" is used as an effective tool for emphasis.

Here's a useful test of whether something is a fragment: add "It is true that" to the beginning of a phrase; if it still makes sense, it's a full sentence. If it doesn't make sense, it's a fragment. "It is true that how ironic," for instance, doesn't make sense. It's helpful to deliberately choose, on a case by case basis, whether or not to use a fragment. Fragments appear most often in creative non-fiction and advertising and least often in academic writing, where they are generally viewed as serious errors.

**Comment [S4]:** While academic writing generally calls for smooth transitions that refer back to the thesis and previous paragraph, creative non-fiction allows writers to use extra space (or, if they prefer, an asterisk) to indicate a change in scene.

**Comment [S5]:** Note the repetition of "line" and the shift in meaning. While inexperienced writers often think creative non-fiction is a simple genre that just involves telling a story, it is actually a highly complex genre requiring much craft on the part of the writer.

This time I take the stairs up to the room. Gingerly I make it step by awkward step up the four flights. When I come through the door everyone is there.

"Hey!" they greet me.

"Hi." Shit, I better sound happier.

"What's wrong?"

Deny. Deny. DENY.

"Nothing."

"There has to be something. Come on, you look really upset."

"I'm fine. I mean, I feel much better now. I'm tired though. Just go to dinner without me."

They really don't need to know. It's not that important.

**Comment [S6]:** This section is an excellent example of perhaps the most important piece of advice for anyone writing creative non-fiction: "show, don't tell." In other words, in this genre writers tend to make points implicitly rather than explicitly; they use details to allow readers to figure things out for themselves. This writer, for example, could have omitted the dialogue and instead just told us, "I had friends who cared about me. Unfortunately, I minimized my problem and did not take advantage of the support they could have given me." Luckily for us as readers, the writer allows us to infer this point rather than coming right out and telling us.

Note that in most other genres, including most academic genres, the opposite advice holds true; readers expect to be told what the point is, and they often get frustrated if it is not explicitly stated. This is one reason writing is so difficult; readers expect different conventions to be followed in different genres. To get a sense of which conventions are followed in which genres, it helps to read several examples of a genre before writing in that genre.

Alex Perry

# Turning Tides

2007 Award for Excellence in Creative Non-Fiction

*This creative non-fiction essay deliberately manipulates what readers know and when they know it, holding back a key piece of information until the very last paragraph. As you are reading this essay, consider the effect of this delayed disclosure. Is this a strategy you might want to use when writing in this genre? In what cases might you want to use delayed disclosure and in what cases might you not want to?*

*You may also want to consider the way that Perry shows rather than tells. Instead of coming right out and telling us that "my problem was very difficult to live with," he shows us; he lets us infer this idea. As you're reading his essay, find a few passages where Perry shows rather than tells. What does he gain by using this strategy?*

*Also worth considering is Perry's recognition of complexity, as illustrated by the last sentence of the essay. In most genres, readers generally prefer writing that recognizes complexity. Because the world is indeed complex, recognizing that complexity bolsters your credibility as a writer, while ignoring it can undermine your credibility. To recognize complexity in academic writing, you'll want to present nuanced arguments that recognize and address potential objections rather than making simple pro or con arguments. Similarly, in creative non-fiction, simple pat narratives can leave readers feeling that "that wouldn't really happen." As you're reading Perry's piece, consider how you might be able to recognize complexity in your own writing.*

My eyelids shoot open in unison with the shade moving up quickly past my window. The beams of sunlight find their way to me, giving me an excuse to close my eyes again. What a beautiful day it must be, and after a rejuvenating twelve hours of sleep, one should be able to take full advantage.

I am wide awake, but I'm tired, still tired, enough to add another twelve hours to the count. Whoever did me the kind favor of opening my shade leaves the room while trying to make as much noise as humanly possible in a five-yard walk, but my sleeping powers cannot be overcome by such an attempt. My eyes threaten to close again, leading me into another escape, but the alarm placed on the stand next to me has different plans. The noise is low at first, but soon it will be unfathomably loud, and equally unpleasant. My hand quickly finds its way to the button on top, ending the noise in an instant, but it does not return to my side. Instead, it hovers over the clock, frozen in a position of terror as I feel all control slip away. The dark figure next to me is pressing the cold steel of his blade against my head, and I try not to move, only focusing on meeting his demand, whatever it is.

"Again," he demands in a familiar hiss.

I comply, and without a moment's hesitation, my hand drops down once again on the clock as I push the button a second time.

Running will not be necessary this morning, of course. He will find me no matter where I disappear to, and there will be no mercy; more demands will come. Though it will seemingly make no difference at all, in this moment when I am a prisoner, I am able to pause, and it is in this moment that I choose to reflect.

It was not always like this. There was a time when he was not around. If my memory serves me correctly, he was non-existent during my childhood. Perhaps I was simply not looking closely enough, and there he was around every corner, watching and waiting for the right time to strike.

Like any truly intelligent nemesis, he befriended me first, and offered to keep things on track if I simply completed his tasks. I touched a railing in my house. "Could you touch it three more times please?" he would pleasantly ask. "Possibly four more now?" he continued. "Okay, twelve times should seal the deal." It was nothing.

So how did it come to this? Lying here frozen and at his mercy as he threatens to end my existence. I prefer not to dwell on the journey, and I keep it tucked away safely in the back of my mind.

I meet every demand he throws my way now. However, I cannot help but notice the fear in his eyes this morning. Something is different, and he is aware of it. I know exactly what it is, and it is mine to keep far away from his line of sight. It is in fact my only weapon against him, and if I were to hand it over, my hope would be attached to it, and along with that, my life. In the moment of reflection that occurred as my hand fell onto the clock for a second time, I made a journey. In that moment, as the memory of a time before he existed entered my mind and journeyed into my heart, I remembered not only a time without him, but also a feeling empty of all worry. It is a feeling that is worth holding onto. It is a powerful weapon and I look forward with great anticipation to using it against him.

I hope that as I go through my morning routine while meeting his demands, he notices the determination in my eyes. I want him to know his end is coming. I want him to see the train coming from miles away before it crushes him.

He follows me downstairs where I sit with my mother for breakfast. She knows that he is there too, always. He has a name; OCD is what she calls him. She asks me if I would get something for her out of the basement that she needs for school, and I tremble. I sat down at this table with confidence, but walking into his lair is suicide. I stand up, unbelieving of what I am doing, and walk slowly toward the door leading to the basement. The cold steel once again presses against my head. I know I will not do this. I will make up an excuse that she will see through, and kindly put up with. He is closer now, closer than ever to ending all that I know, and placing my life on a track that only knows downhill. Closing my eyes, my hand reaches up and grasps the freezing lock, and I turn it. After a snap, I open my eyes. His presence seems to have faded. I look to my right, and to my dismay, there he is. Strange, however, is that he is a more than ten feet away, and his face is one of confusion. Next, I open the door, and in less than a second he is out the window, freezing in the cold winter morning. The feeling is back, the one I found again, but this time it is real. I look down the stairs and into the basement, and wonder how long this will last.

Jacqueline Blute

# Forced

*This piece of creative non-fiction makes excellent use of framing; as you read, pay special attention to the way Blute opens and closes the essay. How would the essay be different if Blute had written it as a straight chronological narrative rather than as a flashback?*

*Also consider the subtle foreshadowing that Blute intersperses throughout the piece. How does this foreshadowing affect you as a reader?*

*You may want to discuss the foreshadowing and framing in class, along with the general effect of the piece. Do you find this essay to be powerful? Why or why not? Is Blute using any strategies that you might want to use in your own writing?*

It's been a year and a month since I met him; I'm standing in the bathroom now, door locked, hands shaking, thinking to myself, how could it have come to this? How did it get this far? Is it my fault? I had to sit down, slowly close my eyes, and let the tears fall.

The summer I met him was hot; my skin was suntanned from long hours at the beach and my hair blonde with highlights from squeezing lemon juice in it. The weather outside still felt like summer. Perhaps because of the heat, I insisted on wearing a skirt that day, even though the ice skating rink was cold. The rink looked slightly run-down, yet optimistic with the sight of children learning to skate for the first time; there was a gleam in their parents' eyes as their children tiptoed across the ice eventually falling, but with a smile. I would visit my friend Amanda when she was at the rink, which was almost all the time. She was entered in a skating competition that day, and as a loyal friend I went to support her.

Only moments after I went through the glass door I saw Amanda all ready to go. We started talking, and I wished her good luck. "Hi," a suave voice came from behind me, "Amanda, is this a friend of yours?" Now, I knew a lot of people that worked at the rink, but this was the first day that I had ever met Robert Tansey. Everyone knew him as Robbie. I noticed that he was not very tall, but he did have a nice build. He had short brown hair and wore an Eastham firefighter baseball cap. He was an average junior that attended high school in a neighboring town, and also happened to work at the rink. Amanda introduced us, and for the rest of the day I noticed him, noticing me. I thought nothing of it.

When I got home that evening I signed on my screen name on the computer, put up an away message, and had dinner with my family; it was just another average day. That night I called Amanda on the phone: "You did!? You won second place? I'm so proud of you!" I exclaimed, as she sounded so ecstatic. I was in my own world then, so simple minded, not knowing much about the world outside. I went over to my computer to see if I had received any messages; usually I didn't get any. When I looked at the screen I had received a message from Tansey123. The message said, "Hi, this is Robbie the boy you met at the rink. I just wanted to let you know how beautiful I thought you were today and hope to see you again soon." I was taken aback by his message. I thought to myself, a boy likes me? Me of all people? Beautiful? How insecure I was, and the thought of someone thinking that I was beautiful made me feel like I was actually some-one special.

School started up again. Leaves falling and changing colors, no more sandals, warm sweaters, the football team undefeated, it was the beginning of fall. The first bell rang and I quickly walked to class and sat down next to Amanda. "We're not freshmen any-more!" Amanda cheered. She was right; now we were sophomores. It still felt the same. I told Amanda about the message, and she asked me if I wanted to come over after school. Whenever she said, "come over," she usually meant to the rink. I hesitated, thinking of the boy who thought I was beautiful. Amanda had convinced me, though, saying she could get us free snacks from the snack bar.

After school Amanda's mom picked us up and brought us over to the rink. The doors had not yet been cleaned; children's handprints glowed on the glass from the family skate time that had ended only minutes before we walked in. Amanda and I went over to the snack bar; we each got a few snacks and sat down to start homework. "Hi." That same voice from before, behind me again. This time I turned around and said "hi" back. Robbie then sat down. We talked for hours, literally. It was getting late and I called my dad to have him come pick me up. Robbie asked me for my cell phone number and I reluctantly gave it to him. What would I say if he called me ever? I was never really interested in Robbie at first. He was just that boy that was interested in me. My friends had mixed feelings about him too. We did not go to school with him so we didn't know too much about him. Amanda told me he was nice enough, but still I didn't know.

That night I was comfortable just sitting in my computer chair, relaxing in my sweatpants and t-shirt. All of a sudden, Robbie instant messaged me and I felt as if I was wearing an itchy dress and wobbling in high heals. How could just a regular guy make me feel so uncomfortable? It was not a bad feeling; I just did not know how to react around a guy that was interested in being more than just friends. To my surprise, Robbie and I had a very extensive conversation. We talked about our interests, family, and friends, anything that we could think of. He was easy to talk to, especially when he made comments such as "you looked so pretty today" and "I really love your eyes." I hadn't been given lines like that before; I took them as sincere. I used to have a lot of trust in people, almost everyone.

A few months later I went to the rink for rock night, where Amanda and I were DJs. Robbie also worked that night. He came over and talked to me, and again we talked for hours until Amanda's mom, who managed the rink, busted his chops for not taking out the trash. Robbie gave her a withering look, and stormed off in a rage to do work.

Amanda noticed that he really liked me, and how I seemed to feed into that. It was about 9:50 and rock night was coming to an end. Everyone would return their skates to the rental shop, they'd buy their last snack at the snack bar, and off they'd go. Robbie always seemed to just creepily appear. "Hi Jackie, I have to go now, but I want to ask you on a date this Saturday, and I'm not taking no for an answer." He smiled. I panicked. I felt pressured into saying yes, so I did.

The whole ride home I wondered to myself, why did I say yes to the date? Did I like him? I didn't want to go. Should I tell my parents? I am their first child; they rarely let me do anything and a date would be out of the question. So instead I told them I was sleeping over my friend Andrea's house. I decided that telling my parents the truth would be an absolutely horrible idea. The reason for sleeping over Andrea's on Friday night would be so that I could leave with Robbie Saturday morning.

That Friday night, Andrea and I spent most of our time laughing and talking about how ridiculous this date would be. Robbie had planned to pick me up at five in the morning to watch the sunrise. I thought about how romantic that was and how uncomfortable I would be. It was still dark when I woke up at Andrea's house. It was very cold out, and I quickly jumped into the shower, the warm water hitting my body and my mind racing with thoughts of how this day would go. At 5:00 a.m. I ran out to Robbie's truck as he rolled into the driveway. His truck smelt of must, and there were dents on the doors. His truck was very old and only had a long bench seat in the middle. This seemed like such an unusual date. It was so cold and Robbie began to drive. The butterflies churned in my stomach. We got to the beach and watched the sunrise. Do I even like this boy? I thought to myself. He looked at me and said, "I wanted to ask you something."

"What is it?" I replied, my throat a little dry, afraid of that one question I hoped he wouldn't ask, at least not this soon.

Robbie cleared his throat and slowly muscled through the words he was about to say: "Well, I've been doing a lot of thinking about you, and I really, well, I just, wanted to know if you'd be my girlfriend."

 The butterflies seemed to have dropped dead in my stomach. My eyes shifted around inside the car, then out the window, squinting at the slow, red and pink rising sun. His body leaned into mine and I couldn't breathe, like the car was filling with carbon monoxide through the heaters and I was suffocating. My hands were clenched together afraid he'd reach for one, causing awkward contact. I was a stiff as if a long board was tied to my back. I just wanted to roll down the window and gasp for breath. The only thing that I could think of was how the rest of the date would go if I said no. This felt like the longest pause, minutes could have gone by in our silence, with him glaring at me. Finally, as if he had asked a million dollar question, I answered him: "Sure." Did I want to say "sure"? I obviously didn't know what I wanted.

We left the beach when the sun was bright in the sky. Of course, Robbie chose to go to Amanda's house; some date, I thought to myself. Amanda was in a skating competition in Natick that day, and this is where the lying began in earnest. My mom had called my cell phone and drilled me with a million questions. None of the answers I gave to her were true. I couldn't believe I was lying, but it was just so easy. This day seemed to last forever. Such a cold winter it was, frost forming every morning now. Sometimes it would snow, but rarely would it collect on Cape Cod. Robbie seemed to like me more and more, and I did eventually begin to like him.

I could only see him by sneaking around. My life became a lie with my parents; I was afraid to tell them that I had an older boyfriend who drove me places, bought me things, called me his sweetheart. How simple minded I was. Robbie became attached quickly. Sometimes he would show up at my school unexpectedly. I would always see him driving his white truck, just catching my eye before he turned a corner.

Though the winter seemed to drag out, it felt as though spring came out of nowhere. I saw less of Andrea and Amanda and more of Robbie. I noticed things about Robbie, his temper for instance; he had a terrible temper and would get upset over the most insignificant situations. I learned more about how he acted in school, and that not many people liked him there. He was selfish, arrogant, and controlling. Slowly I fell into a trance; even after I learned these things about him I became infatuated.

My mind felt brainwashed at some points. Robbie would make a mistake, yell at me, and I would apologize. He would get frustrated with me, and call me names—names that were no longer sweetheart. He would constantly invite me over just so that we could make out. He would try to go further, but I wouldn't let him. I was still young and innocent.

Spring ended, school got out; I was so relieved that it was summer again. My pale white skin would soon turn to bronze and there would be no more stress over tests and homework. I was free from school, but not from Robbie.

It was a beautiful sunny day on Cape Cod. I decided to call Andrea. Her voice picked up on the other line: "Hello?" Andrea and I knew what a sunny day on the cape meant for us. "Hey, it's me! Look outside, want to go to the mall today?" As residents on Cape Cod we knew that a beach day for tourists would be a mall day for us. Andrea said of course and I began to get ready.

Only moments after I got off the phone with Andrea, Robbie called. "Hey babe, what are you doing today?" Before I could even get two words out of my mouth he asked, "Who are you going with? When? Where? I'll drive us." This was typical for him to call me and harass me like a drill sergeant. Once he found out Andrea and I were going to the mall, he immediately invited himself. I knew he only did this so he could keep an eye on me.

As Robbie roared into the driveway Andrea sighed and we opened the white dented door of his pick up truck. I looked out the back window; the beautiful, warm sun seemed to melt into the ground. Our trip to the mall was more like a blur. Andrea and I felt as if we were being timed in each store, racing the clock that Robbie set. He rushed us out of the mall as quickly as he could to drop Andrea off and spend time alone with me. He had always made me feel rushed with my friends, but I was still clueless, and thought that I really liked him. He made me feel rushed with many things, like he was pushing me into things I did not want to do.

Robbie had a lot of trouble at home, and to get away he had bought a mini pop-up trailer and set it up in his aunt's backyard. He spent a lot of time in the trailer. "I can't wait until I get my own place; just think of how happy we'll be," he would always say. I often thought how weird it was for him to include me into his future. He was my first boyfriend, and I knew he wasn't "the one." He told me he loved me, and I only said it back out of fear. He had such controlling behaviors; he would look at me, his eyes burning with hatred, even though he told me he loved me every day.

It was a little after my sixteenth birthday. I felt so mature now. I got my driving permit, I had a boyfriend, it was summer; I felt like things were going well for me. Even my parents knew about Robbie now, but they didn't know everything; they knew he was a "good friend" of mine and I let it rest at that. They began to trust me more, yet I continued to lie. I would sneak out and see him, telling my parents lies to make him seem better.

Robbie kept taking me to his house, trying to make me do things with him. He would caress my shoulder, and rub my thigh, starting out to be gentle, just cuddling, but eventually closing in like a bear mauling its kill. I wasn't really comfortable around him that way. On a hot summer day in August he told me he wanted to go swimming. I hastily got on my bathing suit, grabbed a towel and some sunblock, announced a quick lie to my family and was off to visit him. He always drove; he told me he felt powerful when he drove. I never looked into these words but soon he would feel even more powerful. He took me to his aunt's house. "Why are we here?" I asked him. "Oh, I just have to pick up a few things for my grandma. How about I show you my trailer," he replied, with a soft smile. I knew he just wanted to go and make out, but I went with him anyway because I did like him. Despite his controlling behaviors and anger problems, I liked him; I was trapped.

He started to kiss me, and we sat on his bed. He pushed me over playfully. His trailer was musty, and dirty. The tables had a thin layer of discolored yellow mold. The curtains were of little boats, but you could tell the color had worn off from age. The floor was lifting slightly, warped from the heat. A single fan blew from the ceiling in the center of the trailer. Robbie locked the door. He kept kissing me, more and more forcefully. "Are you ready?" he said.

"Ready?" I asked. I knew his question as plain as day, and he knew my answer before he even asked. We had discussed sex before. I told him I did not want to have sex for a very long time, and he told me that he understood. "Are you ready, to have sex?" he asked. I answered no. I didn't want to. He gave me a look—the look that he gave when he asked me on that first date. "I'm not taking no for an answer." I told him I was afraid and that I didn't want to do this. He told me it wouldn't hurt. He kept insisting, and I resisted. No, no, no, no, the words echoed like they had no meaning to him. Before long he had taken me by force; his body was pressed against mine and not even a sound could come from my mouth; only tears could fall from my eyes. I pushed away once and I felt the pressure of him. I felt crushed and broken. No longer was I innocent; he took that from me. Once he pulled back from me, the tears in my eyes made it hard to run away. I ran anyway, I felt so trapped, so helpless, so broken. And here I am now standing in the bathroom, door locked, hands shaking, thinking to myself, how could it have come to this? How did it get this far? I had to sit down, slowly close my eyes, and let the tears fall.

Christina Smith

# Just Another "Carnie"

*In this creative non-fiction essay, Smith uses dialogue in two different passages. As you're reading, ask yourself what the effect of this dialogue is. If you were writing a creative non-fiction essay, how would you decide when to use dialogue and when not to?*

*While dialogue is commonly used in creative non-fiction but only rarely in academic writing, Smith uses another rhetorical strategy that is useful in both types of writing: the antithesis. An antithesis is the juxtaposition of two opposite ideas (i.e., "not X but rather Y," as illustrated by JFK's famous utterance "Ask not what your country can do for you but rather what you can do for your country"). As you read Smith's piece, consider the two antitheses in her last three sentences. Do you find them to be effective? Why or why not? When might you use an antithesis in your own writing?*

The afternoon sun beat down on me. The air felt sticky and I was trying to find a spot where I could stand in the shade. My radio squawked and I listened for a moment. My partner was calling in for a break. I smiled and looked down. We'd taken one too many breaks today I thought. The uniform shirt was made of thick, heavy material and was uncomfortably hot to wear. The only thing I liked about it was the fancy emblem on the front that read "Marshfield Fair Security." I'd been so excited to get the job and was enjoying (almost) every moment of it. The heat was rather a killer today, but for the most part, I really loved the job. I liked watching people and being able to help. It made me feel important and gave me a sense of authority I'd never experienced before. It made me all the more enthusiastic about being a police officer someday. I knew I was just a "rent-a-cop," but I wanted to do my best at this job.

It was the last week of August, and the fair was beginning to die down. I figured a lot of people were leaving because it was so hot. A small wind kicked up and I took a deep breath, enjoying the quick, cool relief. The brief gust carried the all-too-familiar scent of fried dough and vinegar fries. I was craving some ice-cream, but I didn't have enough money. I headed over to the Midway and stood by the ATM sign. This was a nice spot to stand, near the bathrooms in case anybody asked how to get to them and across from the ATM machine. I could see a whole lot from here too. The only problem with this site was that it was directly in the sun. I didn't care anymore though; at this point the sun was so high that there were no shady spots left. I noticed one of the "carnies" walking towards me. I sighed and looked away. These people annoyed me so much. As the youngest female security guard, I was subjected to much of their harassment.

"Boy is it hot out here!" came a voice next to me. It was the carnie. I turned my head, ever-so-slightly in his direction and just nodded, avoiding eye contact. He was airing out his shirt and smiling at me. His teeth were nasty, yellow and half missing—like all the other carnies here. "I'm headin' back to the trailer to take a shower." I smiled. *Good idea.*

"Okay," I replied, with no enthusiasm in my voice. He finally kept on walking. *So, they do clean themselves every once in awhile, that's nice to know,* I thought.

"Ride engineer" and "game operator"—those were the "politically correct" names for them. We just called them carnies, though never in front of them or over the radio. The carnies were a different sort of people. They lived in their own little world, with their own morals (or rather, lack of them). It seems all they did was smoke, drink and just live for the night life. Back at the security office we'd talk and joke about them. They were like the "low-life scum," the bottom of the hierarchy in our "carnival caste system." If I had been an ordinary citizen and overheard the conversations of the security personnel about the carnies, I may have thought them to be harsh or crude. After getting to know the carnies better, though, I didn't feel like I was being a jerk for disliking them so much. They were strange and the older guys gave me the creeps.

There was this one kid in particular, though, that I'd talked to a couple of days ago. I was walking around to the far side of the park where there wasn't much activity, sort of just sweeping through, when I noticed him at the window of a fried dough stand. He asked me how I was doing and we started talking. He told me to come by and he'd give me some free dough. I stopped by there every now and then just to say "hi" but usually didn't stay long, and I never accepted any free fried dough. I love the stuff but his stand didn't look all that sanitary. There were very few people over there so it wasn't patrolled as often. I felt bad for him though. Business was extremely slow in that section and he complained about being bored.

The day passed by and I took a stroll down to the other side to say "hi" to "dough boy" as I called him. He thought the nickname was funny. We had an interesting conversation that evening, and in a strange way, it changed the way I thought about these people. We'd been talking about school. He was going to be a senior.

"Are you planning on going to college?" I asked him.

"I don't know, probably not." His reply didn't shock me, but I was a little surprised. I guess I'd always naively believed that college was something people my age thought a lot about or at least was something they wanted.

"Well, what do you want to be?" I continued. He shrugged his shoulders.

"I don't know, probably just work here." Suddenly, I felt sympathy for this kid. He'd grown up in the carnival all his life. It was all he'd known. He had no direction in life, no great future ahead—he'd been born into the life of a carnie. I wondered if they'd all started out like him. I don't remember much else of what I said, but I don't think it was really important. I didn't get a chance to talk to him much more after that. I was kept busy stationed at different locations, but whenever I got the chance I'd take a walk down there just to say "hi." The last time I remember seeing him he was sitting on a bench taking a smoking break.

It's strange how I could learn so much about life in only a few days. I'd taken for granted that I had a nice home, grew up in a loving family and had dreams and a great future ahead of me. I had a solid idea of where I was going and what I wanted to do. Looking back over those days I'd worked the fair and the different experiences I'd had changed me in a way. It was an eye opener to me, and I feel I understood others better than I ever have before. I never thought myself to be judgmental, but now I try to look at people differently, as fellow human beings. I took the job not really knowing what to expect, and left with not just a paycheck, but a better understanding of myself and those around me. That kid wasn't just another "carnie." He was a person, just like me.

Kristina DiRino

# Class Differences in the Classroom

As a college student, I have been looking back on my time spent in elementary, middle, and high school. After reflecting on this, I realize just how much of an important part of life school is. Not only do students participate academically, but they also attain knowledge concerning life choices that will shape their future and build foundations for their beliefs and morals, which will be a part of them for the rest of their life. With this being true, the topic of social class in education comes into play. Because school is such an influential part of any student's life, social class distinctions have an effect on any student's future. Both teaching methods and resources vary depending on social class and locations of schools, and these class differences in schools play a significant part in shaping a student's future.

> **Comment [S1]:** Here the writer could have said "Students participate academically, and they attain knowledge concerning life choices." Instead, however, she chose to use the "not only...but also" sentence structure, which is a useful tool for emphasis.

The methods through which children are taught play a major role in perpetuating class difference. For example, in Jean Anyon's essay "Social Class and the Hidden Curriculum of Work," she demonstrates the differences in teaching used in schools of varying social classes. Two of these types of schools were working-class schools and executive elite schools. Anyon starts by describing the method of teaching in the working-class school as "following the steps of procedure. The procedure is usually mechanical, involving rote behavior and very little decision making or choice" (197). The author describes the atmosphere as strict and rigid. Children must ask to go to the bathroom and then sign a pass. Children do not get to make decisions for themselves and are taught to listen only to the teacher. Teachers use harsh, brash language when talking to the children, using expressions such as "'Shut up,' 'Shut your mouth,' 'Open your books,' and 'Throw your gum away—if you

> **Comment [S2]:** Note that the thesis makes a clear argument rather than simply stating a fact. (If the writer had said "Many schools are under-funded while others receive much more money," she would have been simply stating a fact.) Making an argument rather than stating a fact is important in many academic disciplines, not just English.

74

want to rot your teeth do it on your own time'" (Anyon 200). Children in these schools are growing up learning to be submissive and follow directions from others. They are being prepared to take part in unskilled blue-collar jobs such as "storeroom and stock room workers; foundry men, pipe welders, and boiler makers; semi-skilled and unskilled assembly line operatives; gas station attendants, auto mechanics, maintenance workers, and security guards" (Anyon 196). It is reflected through the teaching methods that these types of jobs are what these children are expected to attain. They are being taught by teachers to follow orders and have very little opportunity to think for themselves, which is what the jobs they are expected to have entail. The children are underestimated and are not encouraged to make a better life for themselves.

In contrast to the working-class schools, there are the executive elite schools. Teaching is approached from an entirely different perspective where children coming from upper class families and communities are being prepared for rewarding and higher-paying jobs. For example, Anyon describes the way upper-class children are taught:

> **Comment [S3]:** One effective way to introduce a quotation is to summarize what is important about it. (That way, readers know what to look for when they read the quotation.) When your introduction to a quotation is an independent clause (when it could stgand alone as a sentence), use a colon after the introduction to link it to the quotation.

In the executive elite schools, work is developing one's analytical intellectual powers. Children are continually asked to reason through a problem, to produce intellectual products that are both logically sound and of top academic quality. A primary goal of thought is to conceptualize rules by which elements may fit together in systems and then apply these rules in solving a problem. Schoolwork helps one to achieve, to excel, to prepare for life. (205)

> **Comment [S4]:** Note that in MLA format, writers indent quotations longer than four lines. Indented quotations are called "block quotations" and do not require actual quotation marks. To indent a quotation, select it and, on the bottom toolbar in MS Word, click the "Increase Indent" icon (the one with the blue arrow pointing to the right).

In the executive elite schools children are taught to think for themselves. They are regarded as intelligent individuals who are capable of learning on their own and are able to have their own ideas and thoughts. Teachers encourage kids to participate and think for themselves as opposed to telling them what is correct. Teachers also refrain from scolding the students and instead use words of encouragement. Anyon explains, for example, that "The teachers were very polite to the children, and the investigator heard no sarcasm, no nasty remarks, and few direct orders" (208). These two categories of schools are extreme opposites, and Anyon uses them to show the drastic difference between a working-class school and an executive elite school. Anyon's observations are a perfect example of how education plays a part in perpetuating class differences.

Not only do teaching methods affect class differences in schooling, but the unequal allocation of resources further encourage these differences. David Tyack, professor of education and history at Stanford, discusses the many resources that are being denied to under-funded schools:

> **Comment [S5]:** This is a second way to introduce a quotation. Try to avoid "floating quotations," or quotations that aren't introduced. Instead, lead into a quotation with your own words; don't allow it to stand alone as its own sentence. ("Floating quotations" can disorient readers.)

> **Comment [S6]:** This is an effective transition because the first part of the sentence refers back to what the writer has already told us ("given information") while the second part of the sentence previews the sub-argument to be made in this paragraph ("new information"). Putting given information before new information helps orient readers.

All too many schools serving needy children lack staff trained to teach. . . Such schools need the most accomplished teachers, the smallest classes, buildings to be proud of, advanced academic courses as well as remedial ones, social and health services, stimulating after school programs, and a rich curriculum that respects the culture and taps the multiple talents of students. Yet how often do schools with large concentrations of low income and minority students have such resources? . . . so long as school resources continue to reflect the gross inequalities of wealth and income in this country, major achievement gaps will persist between the prosperous and the poor, and too many students will continue to be . . . "thoroughly trained in failure." (Tyack 126)

Schools located in cities where poverty is prevalent tend to compromise children's education due to lack of money. These lower class schools tend to have outdated textbooks and materials, not every child gets his or her own textbook, there is a larger amount of violence, there is less technology such as computers, fewer classrooms, more kids per class, and fewer qualified teachers. Jonathan Kozol, for example, notes that "At Public School 79 . . . the principal says that he is forced to take the 'tenth-best' teachers. 'I thank God they're still breathing,' he remarks of those from whom he must select his teachers" (372). If principals in lower class schools are constantly choosing the "tenth-best" teacher, they're compromising the education of the students. In "Closing the Achievement Gap," Kati Haycock states "We take the students who have less to begin with and then systematically give them less in school. In fact, we give these students less of everything that we believe makes a difference" (8).

Haycock describes exactly what occurs in lower class schools where required materials are not provided due to lack of funds. When comparing these lower class schools to more privileged schools, we see that they have the essential criteria to educate students, such as higher paid teachers, after-schools activities, textbooks for each student, up-to-date books, less violence, and more computers, sports teams, theater and arts programs, and supplies for the children. These children are at a greater advantage. They have all the essential materials to provide a good academic education which will better prepare them for college and future careers. If a child grows up in poverty and cannot attend an upper-class school, the child is automatically put at an unfair disadvantage.

**Comment [S7]:** While the other body paragraphs use evidence to support claims, many readers would find this paragraph even more persuasive since it uses evidence from not one but three sources. When you use evidence from only one source, it's easier for readers to dismiss that evidence; they might believe that whatever quotation, anecdote, or statistic you cite could be a fluke. When you cite *multiple* sources as evidence to support your claims, it's harder for readers to dismiss that evidence.

Note that DiRino also makes it harder for readers to dismiss her evidence by establishing the credentials of one of her sources ("David Tyack, professor of education and history at Stanford, discusses...") Your credibility as a writer rests largely on the credibility of your sources. Because DiRino both establishes the expertise of a source and uses three different sources, this paragraph might provide you with a helpful model to use when you are writing an academic argument.

If children are to succeed in life, they need adequate resources and good teachers to move forward. Children of lower class families are forced to stay in the same social class because the environment provided does not have adequate resources, whereas children in upper class families are able to move forward into respected job opportunities. These influences in school affect children from the moment they step into the classroom and have a lasting impression on them.

# Works Cited

Anyon, Jean. "From Social Class and the Hidden Curriculum of Work." *Rereading America.* Gary Columbo, Robert Cullen, and Bonnie Lisle. 6th ed. Boston: Bedford/St. Martin's, 2004. 194–210.

Haycock, Kati. "Closing the Achievement Gap." *Educational Leadership Magazine* Vol. 58, (2001): 6–11.

Kozol, Johnathan. "Savage Inequalities: Children in U.S. Schools" *Seeing Ourselves: Classical, Contemporary, and Cross-Cultures Readings in Sociology.* John J. Macionis and Nijole Benokraitis. 6th ed. Upper Saddle River: Prentice Hall, 2004. 371–376.

Tyack, David. *Seeking Common Ground: Public Schools in a Diverse Society.* Cambridge: Harvard UP, 2003.

Meghan Gardiner

# To Kill or Not to Kill

2007 Award Winner for Excellence in Researched Writing

*The following essay is a moving and well-researched exploration of the problem of unwanted pets and the challenge of maintaining no-kill shelters. The writer makes it clear that this is a problem she cares deeply about, and uses a wide range of sources in her research—newspaper articles, animal rescue websites, a popular magazine, and a veterinary newsmagazine, as well as her own personal experiences and observations during field research. What effect does the inclusion of personal experience and observations have on you? Do you feel that this is an effective rhetorical strategy for a researched essay?*

Every year, approximately five million animals are euthanized due to overpopulation, which amounts to roughly 56% of all animals who enter shelters (Verdon 37). While there are approximately 5,000 animal shelters nationwide, it is estimated that only about 800 of them are no-kill shelters (Hewitt 100). In this paper, I will address the issue of euthanization and what can be done about this problem while focusing on no-kill shelters. This is a topic that I feel quite passionate about and hope that someday I will be able to solve some of the problems that are addressed in this paper.

Thousands of animal shelters nationwide euthanize healthy animals. Each shelter that euthanizes animals due to overpopulation has their own policies and procedures that they follow. For instance, most shelters have a limit as to how long they will board a pet before it is euthanized. California's policy is just six days and, shockingly, some states euthanize an animal within hours of he or she being dropped off at the shelter. Right here in Massachusetts, the Massachusetts Society for Prevention of Cruelty to Animals has seven shelters which take in about 250,000 animals a year with a single shelter taking in as many as 1,000 animals a month (MSPCA). They simply do not have the room for all these animals and a majority of them are put to sleep. Most of the previous owners have no clue that this is what goes on when they can no longer keep their beloved pet. So, why does America have to euthanize so many animals every year? Well, there are many factors that play into this. First and foremost, many people do not spay or neuter their pets. This is the main issue that is causing the pet overpopulation crisis. In addition, there is not enough funding to take care of all these animals and there is simply not enough room for shelters to provide a temporary home for every animal.

Unfortunately, I know all too well about euthanization. In December, I will have been a volunteer at the Animal Rescue League of Southern Rhode Island for a full year. Every week I go to the Animal Rescue League for about three hours to help out. I love playing with the cats and help out with any tasks that need to be done. I have a lot of personal insight on how the shelter is run and understand that the process of running a shelter is very difficult.

This past Saturday I went to the Animal Rescue League to volunteer. This day was just like any other day at the shelter—it was chaotic. There were a million things going on at once and the staff members were running around as usual. Everyday there is much to be done at this no-kill shelter. Some of the many tasks include cleaning cat cages, which takes well over two hours, feeding the animals specific food based on the particular animal's needs, showing the animals to possible adoptive parents, answering tons of phone calls, and taking care of special needs such as distributing medications.

Saturday was a very sad day at the shelter. About thirty minutes after I arrived, Megan, the manager, and a new staff member walked in looking very sad. A young beagle at the shelter named Lucky had heartworm and could barely breathe. The pair had taken him to an animal hospital and the vet there decided to keep him overnight; she said that if he wasn't better in a few hours, he would probably never get better. He was suffering and in pain but he had a chance of survival. The saddest part of the situation was that Lucky needed an oxygen tent treatment that would cost over $1,000, money the animal shelter simply could not afford (Gardiner).

While the animal shelter that I volunteer at is a no-kill sanctuary, there are far more shelters in Rhode Island and across the nation that aren't. The no-kill movement was pioneered in San Francisco in 1994 and since the beginning of the movement, the number of animals entering shelters is down 62% (Szabo 1).

No-kill shelters can be very good in many ways but also have their downsides. One good thing is that America is on its way to being a "no-kill nation." In the 1980s, over seventeen million animals were euthanized compared to today's rate of about five million annually. This means that altogether euthanasia rates went down 70%. The no-kill movement has initiated sparing of thousands of animals' lives and it is very important that we keep the rate of euthanization from increasing. While some states euthanize more animals then others, New Hampshire has the lowest euthanasia rate in the country. The way in which NH is able to have this honor is by charging a $2 surcharge on dog license fees so that they can provide significantly reduced spaying and neutering to pets of low-income families (Szabo 1). Like NH, there are many other states that are trying to reduce euthanasia rates as well.

The downside to no-kill shelters and the reason why we do not have a no-kill nation is due to lack of funding. San Antonio's no-kill shelter called Animal Friends knows all to well about too little funding. Through an article I read in a San Antonio newspaper titled "Lack of Funds May Force No-Kill Animal Shelter to Close," I learned that Animal Friends will only be able to run two or three more months with the funds that they have. Last year alone, the shelter spent over $76,000 in expenses and this year they are currently nearing $61,000 in expenses. Animal Friends is the temporary home to forty dogs and thirty cats that are housed in 1800 square feet, but, like many other no-kill shelters, they must turn down animals simply because they do not have the room (Budge 10). Unfortunately, there are many other no-kill shelters that are in the same position as Animal Friends. Just recently, Virginia SPCA spent $7 million on a no-kill shelter, money that most non-profit shelters simply do not have. The way in which many no-kill shelters receive money is though adoption fees, fundraisers, and its members; most of them receive no local, state, or national funding (Szabo 1).

Aside from the issue of money, there are many different ways that a no-kill shelter can be successful in adopting out animals. One way that many are successful is by bringing sheltered animals out in public, such as to community and shelter events or for a walk around town. This helps raise awareness about the shelter and may lure some people into the shelter. In addition, many shelters accept volunteers. By doing this, the shelter is able to provide more attention to the animals and more importantly, socialize problematic and disobedient animals. Having volunteered in a shelter, I have seen firsthand how an animal can change his or her behaviors just from receiving a little extra TLC. Also, it is said that the most successful shelters are selective in choosing owners for pets that are adopted out. By being selective, there is less of a chance that the animal will be returned back to a shelter at some point in his or her life (Szabo 1).

For this project, I decided that I wanted to know more about no-kill shelters in Rhode Island. I wanted to see for myself how big of an issue euthanization in America is and relate my research findings back to my own state. Through the website petfinder.com, I discovered that there are over thirty-five animal shelters in Rhode Island and that only about ten of them are no-kill shelters, which was not surprising to me. Through this website, I found out that every shelter has an adoption fee but also charges a spay/neuter deposit fee that is returned to the adoptive parents once they can prove the animal has been altered. Other shelters automatically neuter or spay an animal before it leaves the shelter. The neuter or spay deposit is usually around $25, but some shelters charge up to $60. I found that the no-kill shelters were the shelters that had the highest adoption fees and neuter/spay deposit fees. This makes sense because they need to receive more funds than do kill-shelters because a majority of them receive no government funding. I feel that all shelters should automatically neuter and spay animals before they are released to new owners because I think this will lead to a lot less euthanizing of future perfectly healthy animals (petfinder.com).

In my opinion, no-kill shelters are really wonderful and are where pets should go if their owners can no longer take care of them. While I stand my ground on this view, there are many people that may disagree with me. Some people feel as though euthanizing animals is the only way to handle pet overpopulation. They feel as though it is wrong for animals to have to sit in cages for months waiting for homes (Hewitt 100). I feel that this will lead to the animal having a good life which is more important then putting him or her to sleep for no reason. I guess that no matter what the case may be, people will always find flaws in a plan to change the way animals are treated. However, I feel that if I am persistent enough I will reach my end goal, which is to make Rhode Island the first no-kill state in America. As you know, the first step to solving this problem is spaying and neutering, so, I now leave you with TV legend Bob Barker's famous words: "Help control the pet population, have your pets spayed or neutered."

# Works Cited

Budge, Rose Mary. "Lack of Funds May Force No-Kill Animal Shelter to Close." *San Antonio Express-News*, STATE&METRO ed., 29 Aug. 2006: C10. *LexisNexis*. Bridgewater State College, Bridgewater. 6 Nov. 2006 < www.lexisnexis.com>.

Gardiner, Meghan. "Animal Shelter Observation." Bridgewater State College, 2006.

Hewitt, Bill. "Should Strays Be Killed?" *People* 6 Nov. 2006: 99–100.

"Petfinder.Com: Adopt a Homeless Pet." *Petfinder.Com*. 2006. 9 Nov. 2006 <http://search.petfinder.com/search/search.cgi>.

Szabo, Liz. "Kinder, Gentler Animal Shelters." *USA Today* 26 July 2004: D1. *Academic Search Premier*. EBSCO. Bridgewater State College, Bridgewater. 1 Nov. 2006 <www.ebsco.com>.

"The MSPCA: One of the Nation's Oldest Voices for Animals." *MSPCA Angell*. 2006. 9 Nov. 2006 <www.mspca.org/site/PageServer?pagename=aboutus_History_MSPCA_Angell>.

Verdon, Daniel R. "Sheltered." *The Newsmagazine of Veterinary Medicine* 37: 28. *Academic Search Premier*. EBSCO. Bridgewater State College, Bridgewater. 26 Oct. 2006 <www.ebsco.com>.

Kendra Maksy

# United States' Policy on Music Downloading

2007 Award for Excellence in Persuasive Writing

*This essay sets up a problem-solution argument. Notice how the writer introduces her argument and clearly articulates her thesis. How well does the writer support this thesis? Does the author take into account counter-arguments? If so, how effectively does she address them? Discuss the author's use of sources. Would a wider variety of sources strengthen the author's argument?*

The United States Federal Copyright Laws are meant to protect the rights of musicians or artists while also maintaining the rights of listeners who benefit from the music they create. But some of the laws that are meant to maintain the rights of listeners are doing just the opposite. While it is fair for the United States Copyright Office to declare the copying and selling of music for profit unlawful, it is unfair to also declare that it is unlawful for users to share music that they have previously purchased, with no intention of profit. Users who file share are not making any profit, they are simply sharing files. Users should have the right to share music that they have purchased with others if they choose to do so.

The US Copyright Law states that "Federal law protects copyright owners from unauthorized reproduction, adaptation, performance, display, or distribution of copyright protected works" (U.S. Copyright Office). This generally means that you cannot take another person's music and distribute copies. So if you purchase a CD from the mall, you are legally allowed to make a copy for yourself, but if you sell a copy to another person you are breaking the US copyright law. If you are convicted of doing so, you could face up to five years in prison and $250,000 in fines.

The US also has a Federal Anti-Bootleg Statue that "prohibits the unauthorized recording, manufacture, distribution, or trafficking in sound recordings or videos of artists' live performances" (U.S. Copyright Office). This act means that you cannot lawfully record a copyrighted work and distribute it; also you cannot lawfully put the

83

recording on the internet to be sold. If you are convicted of breaking this law, you could also face up to five years in prison and $250,000 in fines.

The last important copyright law is the No Electronic Theft Act, also called the NET Act. This Act states that "sound recording infringements can be criminally prosecuted even where no monetary profit or commercial gain is derived from the infringing activity. . . . Additionally, the NET Act amended the definition of 'commercial advantage or private financial gain' to include the receipt of anything of value, including receipt of other copyrighted words (as in MP3 trading)" (U.S. Copyright Office). This act means that if you are distributing or copying music for free, you can still be convicted of copyright infringement. It also means that any sharing or trading of music files on the internet is also a violation of copyright laws, even if there is no profit involved. Penalties for violation of this act are, again, up to five years in prison and $250,000 in fines.

A lot of people do not know what these laws actually are and that is why there is so much confusion about music downloading. There are other laws not mentioned about music downloading and all of the information can be overwhelming. It breaks down like this: there are some laws passed in reference to music copyrighting that protect the material of artists, and then there are laws that take away rights of listeners. The US Copyright Law and the Federal Anti-Bootleg Statue are both laws that protect the copyrighted material of artists while still remaining fair to listeners. Both laws deal with gaining profit from copying or bootlegging copyrighted music or videos. These activities are obviously criminal acts and therefore the laws are just. It is the third law mentioned, the No Electronic Theft Act that goes too far. The NET Act was created to protect artists' material on the internet, but this Act is violating the rights of listeners. The NET Act is unfair to users who want to share CD or MP3 files that they have previously purchased with others for no monetary gain. If you buy music, online or in the record store, you should be able to share it with others.

When it comes to music downloading from the internet, there are two things that make copyright laws impractical. The first is that is almost impossible to enforce these laws. Police officers cannot just start to search computers; they need warrants which they cannot obtain without probable cause (Herche). Electronically it is almost impossible to track and record music file downloads, and this type of evidence is not usually accepted in court (Herche). It is almost impossible because recently record companies have found a way to invade the privacy of users in order to "crack down" on music downloading. The *Boston Globe* published an article in March of 2007 explaining that, "The Recording Industry Association of America [The RIAA] has opened one of its biggest assaults yet on illegal file swapping with warning letters to 13 colleges, including the University of Massachusetts at Amherst, asking them to identify on-campus file swappers who the industry intends to pursue for copyright violations" (Bray D1). The *Globe* continues to explain how the recording industry plans to write to many other college campuses and sue many more students (Bray D1). The reason that college campuses are an easy target is because a lot of students participate in file sharing and because, unlike home computers, they are connected to their college's network and the college can track their file sharing activity and report back to the RIAA. Not only is this a violation of the students' privacy but music downloading has not stopped, it has in fact increased by 67 percent from last year according to the research firm Nielsen Sound-Scan (Bray D1). Despite the facts the RIAA continues to persistently punish students.

The second reason why copyright laws are impractical is because a user usually cannot tell when they are downloading music that is legal or music that is copyrighted. Some music is not copyrighted and therefore not protected by US Copyright Laws and can be downloaded legally. In December of 2006, 80 million music files were downloaded legally while 466 million music files were downloaded illegally (Bray D1). The problem is that it is almost impossible for the average person to know if the music they are downloading is legal or illegal. "A music search is conducted based on title or artist and a download occurs with the user completely oblivious to the legal status of the file they are downloading" (Herche).

A lot of people who are convicted of downloading music illegally are parents whose minor children downloaded illegally either unknowingly or without their parents' consent. Parents like, Robyn Werry who was interviewed by the *Boston Globe* because she was sued in 2006 by the RIAA for illegal downloading (Bray D1). Robyn is a 45 year old who works as a nurse in Rhode Island (Bray D1) and her children were downloading music they didn't know to be copyrighted. In her *Globe* interview Robyn said, "We certainly are not copyright thief types . . . and they [the RIAA] are going to go after the parents of these kids and take all of their money" (Bray D1). Because the RIAA usually settles about half of their suits for around $4,000 each, Robyn was advised to settle (Bray D1). "I'm giving them my daughter's college money," she said (Bray D1).

An argument that the record companies use to back up their law suits is the argument that they are losing money because of internet file sharing. This is far from the truth. Not only is the RIAA gaining money from all of their legal suits, there are no statistics to prove that they have lost significant amounts of money because of file sharing. In fact, the RIAA has figures that state just the opposite. In 2004 the amount of consumer purchasing trends based on genre was 23.9 million for rock, 12.1 million for hip-hop, and 10.4 million for country (Consumer Purchasing Trends). In 2005 the amount of consumer purchasing trends based on genre was 31.5 million for rock, 13.3 million for hip-hop, and 13 million for country (Consumer Purchasing Trends). In just one year each genre had increased by millions. Another popular argument is that artists are losing money. However, the artists are paid by the record company before their album is ever released. So, the artists have already been paid even before the public has any knowledge of their new album, and way before any of their new songs are available to be shared on the internet.

So what can be done to fix the injustices of music downloading? We need to find a way to protect the material of artists while still giving users the rights they deserve. This can easily be done by getting rid of the No Electronic Theft Act while keeping the US Copyright Law and the Federal Anti-Bootleg Statue. By doing this the United States Copyright Office would be keeping the laws that protect the material of artists while removing the law that takes away the rights of listeners. If the US cannot remove the NET Act entirely, they could always alter the law to make it clear that file sharing is legal whether it is copyrighted or not as long as there is no monetary gain involved. If there is no profit then there is no reason why sharing should not be legal. If this were done, we would all benefit from the freedom to share the music that we purchase and the release from constant legal suits against students and families by the Recording Industry Association of America.

# Works Cited

Bray, Hiawatha. "Record firms crack down on campuses." *Boston Globe* 08 Mar 2007, natl. ed.: D1.

Herche, Cody. "'Illegal' music downloading." *legal redux*. 21 July 2006. 20 Mar 2007 <http://ledux.blogspot.com/2006/07/illegal-music-downloading.html>.

RIAA, "Consumer Purchasing Trends." *Press Room*. RIAA. 20 Mar 2007 <http://www.riaa.com/news/marketingdata/purchasing.asp>.

U.S. Copyright Office, "Copyright Law of the United States." *Copyright*. 18 Mar 2007 U.S. Copyright Office. 20 Mar 2007 <http://www.copyright.gov/title17/>.

Yvonne Estabrooks

# Manatee "Preservation" in the State of Florida

*The following essay sets up a problem-solution argument about the plight of the manatee. Using a variety of electronic sources, including newspapers, the humane society and* National Geographic *magazine, the author first persuades readers that there is a problem with manatee preservation and then offers several avenues for addressing this problem.*

*Although all scholarly essays use citations, the ways these citations are used may differ somewhat from discipline to discipline. Given the scientific subject matter for this essay, the author is using an approach to citation that echoes scientific style: she chooses not to introduce most of her sources with a signaling phrase which would identify the source's authority (for example,* Dr. John Smith, a noted biologist with the Smithsonian Institution, has observed that...). *Since these signals are missing from the text, the reader must turn to the Works Cited page to gauge the credibility of her sources. Examine her Works Cited page: how many of her sources have .gov or .org addresses? Is the authority of her sources generally self-evident? Note, too, that this author uses very few direct quotations in her text, preferring instead to paraphrase the material. How does this use of paraphrase affect you as you read the essay?*

Manatees are large grey marine animals, often referred to as sea cows, which are only capable of reaching speeds of 3 to 5 miles per hour (Walker). This innocent creature, which has no natural enemies, is victim to humans and the natural world alike. Each year a considerable number of manatees are killed from preventable causes, but insufficient action is being taken to protect them. In June 2006, the state of Florida downlisted the status of the manatee from "endangered" to "threatened." While the Federal Endangered Species Act still holds the manatee under its protection, there is still considerable unrest about the effect this decision will have on the species. The consequences of this downlisting may be severe, and it is estimated that the effect will be so profound it will not be long before the manatee is put right back up on the endangered species list ("Federal Laws").

According to the North Florida Field Office, the manatee population is growing at a steady rate: "Based on published data for survival rates, reproduction, and population growth, the Upper St. John's River and Northwest Florida sub-populations are growing rapidly and doing very well. The Atlantic Coast sub-population is probably stable" (Manatee Recovery Fact Sheet). Yet, in the last five years manatee deaths have increased by 18 percent (Young) and 97 percent of manatees have scar patterns from collisions with boats ("Federal Laws").

It is also important to note that the downlisting is not based on the increasing survival rate of the manatee. The Florida Marine Research Institute "adopted new criteria for listing animals on state endangered and threatened species lists [...]. The definition used by the IUCN (The World Conservation Union) to designate a species as 'critically endangered' would be used by the FWCC (Florida Fish and Wildlife Conservation Commission) to designate a species only as 'endangered,' and the IUCN definition of 'endangered' would be used by the FWCC to place animals on the 'threatened' list"(Young). With this change in definition enacted, boaters will be able to drive at faster speeds and new development will be allowed to surface at current manatee protection areas ("Federal Laws").

The state's choice to change the manatee to a "threatened species" will not change the federal laws, which still consider the manatee endangered. This, however, has been an area of concern: "State and local advocates of the manatee say those federal laws have been of little help to the manatee" ("Federal Laws"). Federal laws can only be as good as the enforcement is. It is a well known fact that boaters can regularly be seen speeding through manatee protection zones, and nothing is done to stop them. Whether it is because of insufficient staff, funding or other reasons, the manatee is not getting the protection it deserves.

It is not just boaters threatening the well-being of the manatee. Manatees in Florida have become a tourist attraction, and as a result, the laws forbidding the feeding and petting of the manatee are not being enforced. The problems from this are twofold. When manatees become domesticated, they lose the ability to distinguish friend from foe. Manatees will go right towards a speeding boat thinking it is a source of food, like any other tourist. The behavior being exhibited across Florida shows the need for stronger action to be taken. According to the *St. Petersburg Times*, "Swimmers chase moving manatees. They block manatees that are seeking food. They wake sleeping manatees with pats and camera strobe flashes" (Behrendt). This action causes much distress to the manatees that can do nothing to stop this unwanted attention. Children and adults attempt to ride the mammas, and baby calves are separated from their mothers.

Rather then a case of rules, it is a case of enforcement. With the new classification system in place there is worry that this problem will only intensify (Young).

The fight for the manatee is not futile, and there are a multitude of actions that can be taken. As a knowledgeable public is the first step in helping protect this species, information about the manatee should be spread throughout communities and public schools. This education effort should teach people about how to treat and handle manatees so that they are respected and not harassed. The laws concerning manatees have to be enforced along with being understood. In manatee protection areas, the speed limit for boaters needs to be regulated and fines should be imposed for any maltreatment of the mammal. There is no reason why the behavior recorded in the *St. Petersburg Times* should be allowed to continue.

Another tool which should be considered in the preservation of the manatee is an apparatus for boats called a prop guard. The prop guard can be attached around the propellers of the boat preventing humans and animals from being shredded by the sharp blades. Reports show that 40 percent of manatee deaths are related to coming in contact with the propellers (Propeller Guard Information). The majority of collision deaths, however, are caused by the force of the boat hitting the manatee while speeding. Critics of the guard argue that the propeller guard impairs the running of the boat. Still, if 40% of manatee deaths could be avoided, this calls for attention.

The debate comes down to a simple question, tourist money or manatees? Manatees are the gentle giants of the sea, a national treasure that it is our job as a people to protect. It is evident that there is not enough being done in the present to save these creatures and with the downlisting of the manatee to "threatened," the problem will simply worsen. With the support of the state government, the legend of the manatee may be able to continue for generations to come.

# Works Cited

Behrendt, Barbara. "Tampa Bay: Manatee Petting: Just Good Fun, or Marine Harassment?" *St. Petersburg Times* 19 Mar. 2006. 26 Oct. 2006 <http://www.sptimes.com/2006/03/19/Tampabay/Manatee_petting__Just.shtml>.

"Federal Laws Won't Protect Manatees, Advocates Say." *Ichthyology at the Florida Museum of Natural History*. 13 June 2006. South Florida Aquatic Environments. 26 Oct. 2006 <http://www.flmnh.ufl.edu/Fish/southflorida/news/federal2006.html>.

"Manatee Info." *Save the Manatee Club*. 26 Oct. 2006 <http://www.savethemanatee.org/man-fcts.htm>.

"Manatee Recovery Fact Sheet." *North Florida Field Office*. 16 Feb. 2005. U.S. Fish and Wildlife Service. 26 Oct. 2006 <http://www.fws.gov/northflorida/ Manatee/manatee-gen-facts.htm>.

"Propeller Guard Information." *Myfwc.com*. Florida Fish and WIldlife Commission. 26 Oct. 2006 <http://www.floridaconservation.org/manatee/prop/>.

Young, Sharon. "Florida and the Feds Get Failing Grades on Manatee Protection." *The Humane Society of the United States*. 24 May 2006. The Humane Society of the United States. 26  Oct. 2006 http://www.hsus.org/marine_mammals/marine_mammals_news/florida_and_us_get_failing_grades_on_manatee_protection.html>.

Walker, Cameron. "Manatee May Lose Endangered Status in Florida." *National Geographic News*. 26 Feb. 2003. 2 Nov. 2006 <http://news.nationalgeographic.com/news /2003 /02/0226_030226_manatees.html>.

Mary Klenowski

# Smoking: A New Discrimination

*The following essay argues that smokers are being discriminated against. Notice how the opening anecdote sets up an effective frame through which the author approaches her argument, while also introducing us to the author's voice. By introducing readers to someone who has experienced this kind of discrimination, the author appeals to our emotion and creates a bridge for understanding.*

*How might you characterize the tone of this essay? How does this tone affect the power of Klenowski's argument?*

*Consider the statement* "After conquering discrimination against religion, race, and sexual orientation, our society is facing a new prejudice." *Does the author's erroneous claim that racial, religious and sexual discrimination have been "conquered" diminish her credibility?*

Anita Epolito had been a model employee. As a receptionist for Weyco, an insurance consulting firm in Lansing, Michigan, Epolito had never had a complaint filed against her. After fourteen years of loyal service, Epolito was fired. Not for slacking on the job, or for showing up late. Anita Epolito was fired for smoking cigarettes, after work, in the privacy of her own home. Howard Weyers, the head of Weyco, and the man who ordered Epolito's termination, complained about the health care costs. Anita Epolito was not on the Weyco health plan. Now, over a year after her release from the company, Anita Epolito is unemployed and smoking more than ever (Safer). Who can blame her? After conquering discrimination against religion, race, and sexual orientation, our society is facing a new prejudice. Discrimination of any kind is a problem, but the real issue is not non-smoker versus smoker. The controversy is employers dictating what employees can and cannot do in their private lives.

In the past few years, there has been an increase in firings of cigarette smokers. It is legal to ban employees from smoking on the job for perfectly sound reasons, such as the increased building insurance and to respect those who cannot or will not tolerate cigarette smoke. Now employers are giving employees an ultimatum: quit smoking, even when not on the clock, or lose your job. There has been a social divide between smokers and non-smokers, but, now, a core issue is coming to the surface. If companies are allowed to fire employees for smoking on their own time, this could open the door for employers to completely control the lives of their employees. What employees do in their private lives is none of their boss's concern, unless it is illegal or affects job performance. Firing employees who smoke cigarettes is a form of discrimination and opens the floodgates for more intrusive "lifestyle clauses."

Why would employers want to let go of good and capable workers just because they smoke? "I don't want to pay for the results of smoking," Howard Weyers told *Medicine Law and Weekly* (Saunders B13). Fair enough. According to the *Journal of Occupational and Environmental Medicine*, smokers cost employers about $3000 more each year than non-smoking employees. Annually, U.S. companies pay $12.7 billion in health care costs for obese employees (Babcock). But according to Lewis Maltby, the head of the National Workrights Institute,

> The problem is lots of things increase your health care costs. Smoking. Drinking. Eating junk food. Not getting enough sleep. Dangerous hobbies. Skiing, scuba diving. If you allow employers to regulate private behavior because it's going to affect health care costs, we can all kiss our private lives goodbye (Safer).

This is not the USSR under Stalin; this is America, the land of the free.

To put a positive spin on the issue, one could say these employers are genuinely concerned about the health and well-being of their employees. Yes, smoking is a dangerous habit, and contributes to many health problems. But chomping too many doughnuts is also a bad habit and leads to obesity. Type II Diabetes, Heart Disease, Hypertension, Stroke, and other conditions are caused by obesity. About 30 percent of the US population is obese. About 60 percent are overweight (Babcock). If overweight and obese employees are protected against discrimination in the work place, then smokers should have the same protection. If employers could potentially refuse to hire or fire anyone who increased health care costs, more than half the population would be unemployed.

Now, the big question isn't if firing employees who smoke is right or wrong, but if it is legal. In the case of Anita Epolito and the three other people fired from Weyco, it was. "…What the employer has done here is legal because Michigan state law doesn't prohibit it," says David Morrison, a partner in the labor and employment group with Chicago law firm Goldberg Kohn. As of now, only thirty states have employment laws that protect some smoker's rights (McAleavy). The issue at hand is not really about cigarettes. Michigan State Senator Virg Bernero says, "This isn't about smoker's rights. It's about worker's rights. It's about the fact that when you punch out of the work place, your time is your own (Saunders, B13)." If employers are allowed to terminate workers who choose to smoke on their own time, soon employees will be forced to live a lifestyle not of their own choice.

Even in our "open minded" society, there is now a stereotype that cigarette smokers are "bad" or low class. One thing that seems to slip non-smokers' minds is that cigarettes are not illegal. Unemployment should not be a consequence of smoking. We do not discriminate against people who choose to eat fatty food and become overweight, or those who choose to have unprotected sex and get sexually transmitted diseases. Therefore, we should not discriminate against those who choose to light up a cigarette. If some employees are allowed to make bad decisions and are protected by law, all workers should have the same protection. If not, then a line has to be drawn, and where do you draw that line? It is wrong not to hire candidates because of the color of their skin, because that's racism, but what if someone has pale skin? Can you refuse to hire them because they are high risk for Melanoma and could potentially raise health care costs? It may sound ridiculous, but even twenty years ago firing smokers sounded crazy.

Once employers are allowed to act like totalitarian dictators, this country will have forsaken its founding values. It is un-American to tell anyone, employee, neighbor, friend, what they can or cannot do in their private lives. Life is all about choices, some are good, and some are bad. But, whatever choice we make is our responsibility and our right. Choosing to smoke is a bad choice, but in the United States we are allowed to make that bad choice. It is not an employer's place to question their workers' personal decisions, including whether or not they smoke. Companies pushing their personal beliefs on employees will not stop with smoking. It will continue until our country is filled with clones of what someone else wants us to be. Sadly, the freedom and individualistic beliefs we value will become a faraway dream.

There are ways to fix this problem. Smokers could be included in the Anti-Discrimination Act, or we could reform health care. Employer-paid health care makes bosses "crazy about your health in ways you don't want," says Bio-ethicist Art Caplan of the University of Pennsylvania (Saunders). An easier approach may be to encourage smokers to quit, which companies are choosing to do. Forcing an addict to quit his or her vice is difficult, and usually does not work. No one can change someone who is not ready to change. However, providing support and incentives help. Anything is better than taking jobs away from people who deserve them. Just ask Anita.

# Works Cited

Babcock, Pamela. "Critics weigh pros, cons of Medicare obesity decision." *HR Magazine* 49.9 (Sept. 2004): 25.

McAleavy, Teresa. "Employers Tell Workers to Kick the Habit." *The Record* 1 March 2005. *Newspaper Source*. EBSCOhost 10 March 2007 <http://library.bridgew.edu:3289/ehost>.

Safer, Morley. "Whose Life Is It Anyway?" *60 Minutes* 30 Oct. 2005. 12 March 2007 <http://www.cbsnews.com/stories/2005/10/28/60minutes/main990617.shtml? source=search_story>.

Saunders, Debra. "Where There's Smoke, You're Fired." *San Francisco Chronicle* 17 Feb. 2005: B13.

Cassie Teixeira

# Obesity and Race in America

*This researched argument offers a critique of Morgan Spurlock's documentary film,* Supersize Me, *by highlighting a population not considered in the film: low-income ethnic minorities. In the first paragraph, the writer builds nicely to the thesis, and then moves into claims, clearly supported by researched evidence, with each claim building on the central argument. Notice how the writer chooses to paraphrase researched material, rather than use direct quotes. Do you feel that this strategy, which allows the writer to maintain her voice throughout the essay, contributes to the persuasiveness of this argument? Or would you have found the argument more persuasive had the writer included direct quotations from the sources instead? How do you make choices about the ways you represent researched material and other voices in your researched arguments and essays?*

Morgan Spurlock's documentary film *Supersize Me* addresses the issue of America's obesity epidemic and its link to the fast-food industry. The film questions who is at fault for the substantial escalation of obesity rates across the country in recent years. Many Americans blame fast-food corporations for the increasing rates of obesity, claiming that their advertising "brainwashes" consumers. Others argue, however, that fast-food corporations' marketing is done in the best interest of their business, not to intentionally hurt their customers. Americans should know better that only each individual can be responsible for his or her eating and exercising behavior. However, could it be possible that some Americans really do not have a choice when it comes to their health? "Supersize Me" addresses obesity in children and the average white, middle-class American adult. Yet, Spurlock fails to take notice of the group of Americans most affected by obesity, those a part of the low-income population, especially ethnic minorities. Consistent evidence has shown that obesity rates of this population compared to non-Hispanic whites are considerably higher.

Studies have proven that race, ethnicity, and socioeconomic status have a correlation with the prevalence of obesity (Kumanyika 188). Several environmental factors in low-income neighborhoods account for this correlation. Food availability, marketing of food, and obstacles to physical activity in low-income neighborhoods are largely responsible for the high prevalence of obesity in ethnic minorities. While it is fair to say that Americans should take responsibility for their own wellbeing, minorities in America are not provided with an equal opportunity to make the appropriate diet and exercise choices necessary to live a healthy lifestyle.

The availability of healthy foods in poor neighborhoods is alarmingly limited. Residents of these areas have fewer sources of healthy foods than residents in wealthier, predominately white neighborhoods. Two to four times as many supermarkets can be found in more affluent neighborhoods across America than in poorer communities (Lee). With fewer grocery stores, fruit and vegetable markets, bakeries, and natural food stores, minorities are not presented with an equal chance for a healthy diet.

Within the few food stores available to poor minorities are even less opportunities for a healthy diet. Studies have shown that food stores in wealthier cities stock healthier food items. In these stores, products that are low-fat or high-fiber, foods that are recommended by professionals as part of a healthy diet, are common. This is not the case in impoverished communities where only limited amounts of nourishing foods are available to purchase (Lee). This evidence shows that despite a minority's desire to live a healthy lifestyle, he or she is set up for failure in American society. Because minorities are not provided with an equal chance for healthy eating, they face an unfair hindrance to their wellbeing.

Reports have shown that poor and predominately black neighborhoods have more exposure to fast-food restaurants compared to neighborhoods of a wealthier, white population majority (Block 212). With more fast-food restaurants per square mile, residents of impoverished black neighborhoods are likely to consume fast food regularly. Within these fast-food and other restaurants, there are actually fewer options for how food can be prepared. Customers in these restaurants may not have the option of having their food baked, grilled, or steamed, healthy preparations that are available in other areas (Lee). Without the choices of salads, fruits, or baked foods, and the prevalence of fried foods, it is certain that consumers are only eating foods that are high in fat and calories, because there are no other options. The convenience of multiple nearby fast-food restaurants is certainly a factor in the high prevalence of obesity in minorities (Block 215). With a number of fast-food restaurants located in low-income neighborhoods, it is understandable that minorities turn to such dining facilities for the quick, inexpensive meals offered just a short distance away from their homes.

The marketing of food products in low-income neighborhoods is associated with the high prevalence of obesity among ethnic minorities compared to the non-Hispanic white population (Lee). Restaurants in low-income neighborhoods are more likely to promote specific, less-healthy menu items to consumers. Studies have also shown that such restaurants are not likely to label menu items to point out healthier food choices

(Lee). Restaurants do adjust the food that they serve according to the nearby residents' preferences, but it is possible that low-income populations do not show a demand for healthier products because of the higher costs (Block 216). The conception that minorities actually prefer less-healthy foods is unjustified. They can only take advantage of what is available to them, which has shown to be limited, regardless of any desire for a healthier diet.

Food is marketed differently based on socioeconomic status because companies in the food industry naturally seek the business of wealthier consumers. Marketers see it more important that higher-income customers are provided with a variety of healthful choices because a happy customer is a loyal customer. Spending more money in low-income neighborhoods to provide better quality food is not beneficial to food industry companies because poor customers are not reliable to increase profits.

The influence of the media also contributes to the higher prevalence of obesity in certain ethnic groups. The second-most advertised products in African American-targeted cable channels and magazines are cookies and candy. While high-calorie cookies are regularly advertised, healthy food advertisements are uncommon in media targeted toward African Americans (Lee). The overexposure and marketing of foods in print advertisements and television commercials targeting the African American population proves to have the impact that the promoters seek: increased consumption of less expensive, yet less-healthy food products.

As fast food consumption increases, physical activity patterns among Americans are either stabilizing or decreasing. This combination of an unhealthy diet and minimal exercise has led to the current obesity epidemic (Block 211). Adequate exercise is difficult to achieve in low-income neighborhoods. Recreational facilities and parks are either inaccessible or unaffordable in these areas ("African-Americans" 14). In impoverished communities, parents are not likely to own a car. Without a means of transportation, participation in sports and other physical activities are not possible for children. Tight budgets are also likely to restrict children from playing organized team sports, where fees are often required for participation (Kumanyika 195). Recreational facilities that are accessible are often in poor, unsafe conditions ("African-Americans" 14). The little attention brought to recreation, an issue that tends to be of little concern for local inner-city governments, is unacceptable. Funding should be put towards restoring run-down public parks and making sports more affordable for poor families. No matter the economic concern, recreation should be a top priority in these communities.

Reduced opportunities for low-income children's physical activity do not only exist based on accessibility and affordability (Kumanyika 199). Concerns for safety in low-income, often high-crime neighborhoods prevent minority children from getting adequate exercise ("African-Americans" 14). With concerns for their children's safety, it is common for parents to actually prefer their children to be indoors rather than on unsafe streets (Kumanyika 195). Because of restrictions on outdoor play, children instead are likely to engage in indoor sedentary behavior, especially watching television (Kumanyika 200). The children viewing television will be exposed to commercials advertising unhealthy foods. In this setting, children are likely to not only be inactive, but also consume high-calorie, high-fat snack foods. Parents' method for keeping their children safe by discouraging outdoor physical activity and instead supporting television watching proves to be a destructive cycle.

As several studies have proven, obesity rates are substantially higher in low-income, ethnic minority populations. Limited access to affordable, quality food products restrains minorities from having a healthy diet. Overexposure of unhealthy foods in nearby fast-food restaurants and found in African-American targeted television shows and magazines is likely to contribute to the high prevalence of obesity in this racial group. Neighborhood constraints on physical activity have a lasting, negative effect on minority children, leading to obesity and other health issues (Kumanyika 199). These environmental factors unique to low socioeconomic status groups explain the disparities of the occurrence of obesity in American adults and children of different ethnicities.

While obesity has increased tremendously in America in recent years, not enough attention has been brought to its effect on ethnic minorities. Much can be done to bring the obesity epidemic to an end. By changing the availability and accessibility of healthy foods and altering the overexposure of unhealthy foods in fast-food restaurants and media, minorities' diets could become more healthful. Changing the foods that minorities are exposed to, providing affordable recreation, and educating minorities about their health are all solutions that would significantly reduce the high prevalence of obesity in ethnic minorities across America.

# Works Cited

"African-Americans Fatter, Less Fit Than Caucasians." *USA Today* Feb. 2005, Your Health: 14.

Block, Jason P., Richard A. Scribner, and Karen B. DeSalvo. "Fast Food, Race/Ethnicity, and Income: A Geographic Analysis." *American Journal of Preventive Medicine* 27.3 (2004): 211–217.

Boardman, Jason D., et al. "Race Differentials in Obesity: The Impact of Place." *Journal of Health and Social Behavior* 46.3 (2005): 229–243.

Kumanyika, Shiriki, and Sonya Grier. "Targeting Intervention for Ethnic Minority and Low-Income Populations." *The Future of Children* 16.1 (2006): 187–207.

Lee, Marlene. "The Neglected Link Between Food Marketing and Childhood Obesity in Poor Neighborhoods." *Population Reference Bureau*. 1 July 2006. 19 Apr. 2007 <http://www.prb.org/Articles/2006/TheNeglectedLinkFoodMarketingandChildhoodObesityinPoorNeighborhoods.aspx>.

*Supersize Me*. Dir. Morgan Spurlock. Perf. Morgan Spurlock, John Banzhaf, Bridget Bennett, et al. 2003. DVD. Columbia, 2004.

# September 2007

| Sun | Mon | Tue | Wed | Thu | Fri | Sat |
|---|---|---|---|---|---|---|
| | | | | | | 1 |
| 2 | 3 | 4 | 5<br><br>Classes begin | 6 | 7 | 8 |
| 9 | 10 | 11 | 12 | 13 | 14 | 15 |
| 16 | 17 | 18 | 19<br><br>Senior Convocation | 20 | 21 | 22 |
| 23<br><br>30 | 24 | 25 | 26 | 27 | 28 | 29 |

# October 2007

| Sun | Mon | Tue | Wed | Thu | Fri | Sat |
|---|---|---|---|---|---|---|
| | 1 | 2 | 3 | 4 | 5 | 6 |
| 7 | 8<br><br>Columbus Day—no classes | 9 | 10 | 11 | 12 | 13 |
| 14 | 15 | 16 | 17 | 18 | 19 | 20 |
| 21 | 22 | 23 | 24 | 25 | 26 | 27 |
| 28 | 29 | 30 | 31 | | | |

# November 2007

| Sun | Mon | Tue | Wed | Thu | Fri | Sat |
|-----|-----|-----|-----|-----|-----|-----|
| | | | | 1 | 2 | 3 |
| 4 | 5 | 6 | 7<br><br>Friday class schedule | 8 | 8 | 10 |
| 11 | 12<br><br>Veterans' Day | 13 | 14<br><br>Monday class schedule | 15 | 16 | 17 |
| 18 | 19 | 20 | 21<br><br>Vacation begins at close of day classes | 22<br><br>Thanksgiving | 23 | 24 |
| 25 | 26<br><br>Classes resume | 27 | 28 | 29 | 30 | |

# December 2007

| Sun | Mon | Tue | Wed | Thu | Fri | Sat |
|---|---|---|---|---|---|---|
| | | | | | | 1 |
| 2 | 3 | 4 | 5 | 6 | 7 | 8 |
| 9 | 10 | 11 | 12 | 13<br><br>Reading Day | 14<br><br>Day classes' final exams begin | 15 |
| 16 | 17 | 18 | 19 | 20<br><br>Day classes' final exams end | 21 | 22 |
| 23<br>30 | 24<br>31 | 25 | 26 | 27 | 28 | 29 |

# January 2008

| Sun | Mon | Tue | Wed | Thu | Fri | Sat |
|---|---|---|---|---|---|---|
| | | 1 | 2 | 3 | 4 | 5 |
| 6 | 7 | 8 | 9 | 10 | 11 | 12 |
| 13 | 14 | 15 | 16 | 17 | 18 | 19 |
| 20 | 21 | 22 | 23<br>Spring classes begin | 24 | 25<br>Winter Commence-ment | 26 |
| 27 | 28 | 29 | 30 | 31 | | |

# February 2008

| Sun | Mon | Tue | Wed | Thu | Fri | Sat |
|-----|-----|-----|-----|-----|-----|-----|
|     |     |     |     |     | 1   | 2   |
| 3   | 4   | 5   | 6   | 7   | 8   | 9   |
| 10  | 11  | 12  | 13  | 14  | 15  | 16  |
| 17  | 18 Presidents' Day—no classes | 19  | 20 Monday class schedule | 21  | 22  | 23  |
| 24  | 25  | 26  | 27  | 28  | 29  |     |

# March 2008

| Sun | Mon | Tue | Wed | Thu | Fri | Sat |
|-----|-----|-----|-----|-----|-----|-----|
| | | | | | | 1 |
| 2 | 3 | 4 | 5 | 6 | 7 | 8 |
| 9 | 10 | 11 | 12 | 13 | 14 | 15 |
| 16 | 17<br>Spring Break begins | 18 | 19 | 20 | 21 | 22 |
| 23<br><br>30 | 24<br>Classes resume<br>31 | 25 | 26 | 27 | 28 | 29 |

# April 2008

| Sun | Mon | Tue | Wed | Thu | Fri | Sat |
|-----|-----|-----|-----|-----|-----|-----|
|  |  | 1 | 2 | 3 | 4 | 5 |
| 6 | 7 | 8 | 9 | 10 | 11 | 12 |
| 13 | 14 | 15 | 16 | 17 | 18 | 19 |
| 20 | 21<br><br>Patriot's Day—no classes | 22 | 23 | 24 | 25 | 26 |
| 27 | 28 | 29 | 30 |  |  |  |

# May 2008

| Sun | Mon | Tue | Wed | Thu | Fri | Sat |
|-----|-----|-----|-----|-----|-----|-----|
| | | | | **1** | **2** | **3** |
| **4** | **5** Spring Day Classes end | **6** Reading Day | **7** Day classes' final exams begin | **8** | **9** | **10** |
| **11** | **12** | **13** Day classes' final exams end | **14** | **15** | **16** | **17** Spring Commence-ment |
| **18** | **19** | **20** | **21** | **22** | **23** | **24** |
| **25** | **26** | **27** | **28** | **29** | **30** | **31** |

# Writing Excellence Awards

The English Department at Bridgewater State College is holding an annual competition to recognize excellent writing in ENGL 101 and 102 courses. Students who submit excellent work may have it published in *Embracing Writing* and may also win a cash award.

Student work will be accepted in the following categories:

1. *Excellence in Expository or Persuasive Writing*—Given to a student paper demonstrating effective use of illustration or evidence to support a thesis.
2. *Excellence in Creative Non-Fiction*—Given to a student paper demonstrating insight and effective use of voice and other literary devices.
3. *Excellence in Researched Writing*—Given to a student paper demonstrating effective use of secondary sources to support an argument or inform readers.
4. *Excellence in Revision*—Given to a student essay demonstrating effective revision strategies. A student entering in this category must submit all drafts (at least two or more) of her or his essay.

*The first place winner in each category will receive $50.* Winning essays, along with other excellent essays, will be published in *Embracing Writing*. Submissions will be accepted both fall and spring semesters, and multiple submissions are allowed. An electronic version of this form can be found at <www.bridgew.edu/wac/WritingAtBSC/StudentPublicationVenues.cfm>. The deadline for submissions is the last day of spring semester. For each submission, please complete this form and email it along with your submission to Dr. Michelle Cox (michelle.cox@bridgew.edu).